Beck Weathers has become a much sought-after speaker before professional, corporate and academic audiences. He lives with his family in Dallas, where he also practises medicine.

Stephen G. Michaud is the author or co-author of nine books, including *The Evil That Men Do* and *The Only Living Witness*.

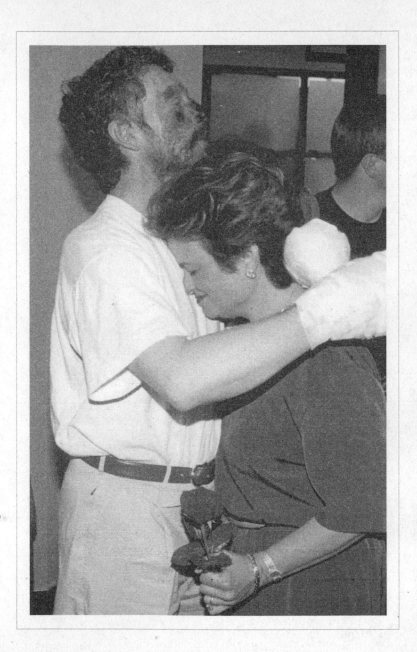

Left for Dead

My Journey Home from Everest

BECK WEATHERS

with Stephen G. Michaud

A *Time Warner* Paperback

First published in the United States in 2000
by Villard Books, a division of Random House, Inc.
First published in Great Britain by Little, Brown and Company in 2000
This edition published by Warner Books in 2001
Reprinted by Time Warner Paperbacks in 2003

A CIP catalogue record for this book
is available from the British Library.

ISBN: 0 7515 3085 9

Photograph on page v © J. Allen Hansley
All other photographs from the author's collection

Printed and bound in Great Britain by
Clays Ltd, St Ives plc

Time Warner Paperbacks
An imprint of
Time Warner Books UK
Brettenham House
Lancaster Place
London WC2E 7EN

www.TimeWarnerBooks.co.uk

For Peach, Beck II and Meg, who gave me the vision to stand and rise from the dead; Madan K.C., who showed us the power of a brave heart; David Breashears, Ed Viesturs, Robert Schauer, Pete Athans and Todd Burleson, for keeping me in the brotherhood of the rope; and in memory of Andy Harris, Doug Hansen, Rob Hall, Yasuko Namba, Scott Fischer, Ngawang Topche Sherpa, Chen Yu-Nan and Bruce Herrod—my deepest sympathy for their families.

Beck at Everest Base Camp.

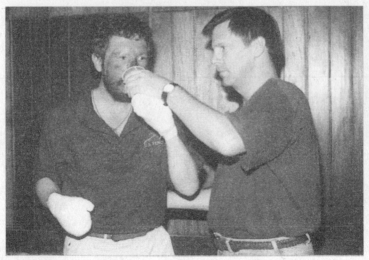

Beck with his brother Dan in Nepal before boarding a plane
to return to the United States.

PART ONE

One

On the evening of May 10, 1996, a killer blizzard exploded around the upper reaches of Mount Everest, trapping me and dozens of other climbers high in the Death Zone of the Earth's tallest mountain.

The storm began as a low, distant growl, then rapidly formed into a howling white fog laced with ice pellets. It hurtled up Mount Everest to engulf us in minutes. We couldn't see as far as our feet. A person standing next to you just vanished in the roaring whiteout. Wind speeds that night would exceed seventy knots. The ambient temperature fell to sixty below zero.

The blizzard pounced on my group of climbers just as we'd gingerly descended a sheer pitch known as the Triangle above Camp Four, or High Camp, on Everest's South Col, a desolate saddle of rock and ice about three thousand feet below the mountain's 29,035-foot summit.

Eighteen hours earlier, we had set out from the South Col for the summit, heartened as we trudged along by a serene and cloudless night sky that beckoned us ever upward until dawn, when it gave way to a spectacular sunrise over the roof of the world.

Then confusion and calamity struck.

Of the eight clients and three guides in my group, five of us, including myself, never made it to the top. Of the six who summited, four were later killed in the storm. They included our thirty-five-year-old expedition leader, Rob Hall, a gentle and humorous New Zealander of mythic mountaineering prowess. Before he froze to death in a snow hole near the top of Everest, Rob would radio a heartbreaking farewell to his pregnant wife, Jan Arnold, at their home in Christchurch. Another sad fatality was diminutive Yasuko Namba, forty-seven, whose final human contact was with me, the two of us huddled together through that awful night, lost and freezing in the blizzard on the South Col, just a quarter mile from the warmth and safety of camp.

Four other climbers also perished in the storm, making May 10, 1996, the deadliest day on Everest in the seventy-five years since the intrepid British schoolmaster, George Leigh Mallory, first attempted to climb the mountain.

May 10 began auspiciously for me. I was battered and blowing from the enormous effort to get that far, but I was also as strong and clearheaded as any forty-nine-year-old amateur mountaineer can expect to be under the severe physical and mental stresses at high altitude. I already had climbed eight other major mountains around the world, and I had worked like an animal to get to this point, hell-bent on testing myself against the ultimate challenge.

I was aware that fewer than half the expeditions to climb

Everest ever put a single member—client or guide—on the summit. But I wanted to join an even more select circle, the fifty or so people who had completed the so-called Seven Summits Quest, scaling the highest peaks on all seven continents. If I summited Everest, I would have only one more mountain to go.

I also knew that approximately 150 people had lost their lives on the mountain, most of them in avalanches. Everest has swallowed up several dozen of these victims, entombing them in its snowfields and glaciers. As if to underscore its vast indifference to the whole mountain-climbing enterprise, Everest mocks its dead. The glaciers, slowly grinding rivers of ice, carry climbers' shattered corpses downward like so much detritus, to be deposited in pieces, decades later, far below.

Common as sudden, dramatic death is among mountain climbers, no one actually *expects* to be killed at high altitude. I certainly didn't, nor did I ever give much thought to whether a middle-aged husband and father of two ought to be risking his neck in that way. I positively loved mountain climbing: the camaraderie, the adventure and danger, and—to a fault—the ego boost it gave me.

I fell into climbing, so to speak, a willy-nilly response to a crushing bout of depression that began in my mid-thirties. The disorder reduced my chronic low self-regard to a bottomless pit of despair and misery. I recoiled from myself and my life, and came very close to suicide.

Then, salvation. On a family vacation in Colorado I discovered the rigors and rewards of mountain climbing, and gradually came to see the sport as my avenue of escape. I found that a punishing workout regimen held back the darkness for hours each day. Blessed surcease. I also gained hard muscle and vastly improved my endurance, two novel sources of pride.

Once in the mountains (the more barren and remote, the better), I could fix my mind, undistracted, on climbing, convincing myself in the process that conquering world-famous mountains was testimony to my grit and manly character. I drank in the moments of genuine pleasure, satisfaction and bonhomie out in the wilds with my fellow climbers.

But the cure eventually began to kill me. The black dog slunk away at last, yet I persisted in training and climbing and training and climbing. High-altitude mountaineering, and the recognition it brought me, became my hollow obsession. When my wife, Peach, warned that this cold passion of mine was destroying the center of my life, and that I was systematically betraying the love and loyalty of my family, I listened but did not hear her.

The pathology deepened. Increasingly self-absorbed, I convinced myself that I was adequately expressing my love for my wife, daughter and son by liberally seeing to their material needs, even as I emotionally abandoned them. I'm eternally grateful that they did not, in turn, abandon me, although with the mountain of insurance I'd taken out against the possibility of an accident, I should have hired a food taster.

In fact, with each of my extended forays into the wild, it became clearer, at least to Peach's unquiet mind, that I probably was going to get myself killed, the recurrent subtext of my life. In the end, that's what it took to break the spell. On May 10, 1996, the mountain began gathering me to herself, and I slowly succumbed. The drift into unconsciousness was not unpleasant as I sank into a profound coma on the South Col, where my fellow climbers eventually would leave me for dead.

Peach received the news by telephone at 7:30 A.M. at our home in Dallas.

Then, a miracle occurred at 26,000 feet. I opened my eyes.

My wife was hardly finished with the harrowing task of telling our children their father was not coming home when a second call came through, informing her that I wasn't quite as dead as I had seemed.

Somehow I regained consciousness out on the South Col—I don't understand how—and was jolted to my senses, as well as to my feet, by a vision powerful enough to rewire my mind. I am neither churchly nor a particularly spiritual person, but I can tell you that some force within me rejected death at the last moment and then guided me, blind and stumbling—quite literally a dead man walking—into camp and the shaky start of my return to life.

Two

The expedition began with a flight from Dallas on March 27. I had to lay over one night in Bangkok before finally arriving in dusty, bustling Katmandu, the capital of Nepal, on the twenty-ninth.

At Tribhuvan International Airport I spied a tall, very athletic-looking fellow waiting in the line to check in. Assuming he was a fellow climber, I approached the fellow and introduced myself. Sure enough, he was Lou Kasischke, an attorney from Bloomfield Hills, Michigan, who'd come to Nepal to climb Mount Everest, too.

Lou and I quickly realized that of all the climbers in our group, we had the most in common. We were both professionals of about the same age and climbing experience, with similar socioeconomic backgrounds. We both were married with kids, and both our wives disapproved of climbing. Over the coming weeks, we would become good friends, as well as tent mates for the expedition.

It took a while to get through customs. Not knowing how

things are done in Katmandu, I'd made the mistake of acquiring a visa in advance, which meant I'd stand in a line at least ten times longer than any of my visaless fellow travelers. I was far and away the last person on my flight to finally get out of the airport.

Outside, I joined up with Lou and a couple of other members of our expedition. A van was waiting to carry us through Katmandu's chaotic traffic to our hotel, the Garuda, an open and airy place and a comfortable haven that clearly catered to a climbing clientele. The walls were covered with posters of the world's great mountains. At the top of the stairway, grinning down on us, was a poster of Rob Hall himself.

Katmandu was a busy, hot and friendly place, with numerous tourists and trekkers, plus us climbers. We enjoyed wandering around the city but did no real sightseeing. I put off buying gifts for the children and the usual peace offering for Peach, incorrectly assuming there'd be plenty of opportunity for that when I returned from Everest.

Two days later, Rob Hall put us into a Russian-built Mi-17 helicopter, an enormous, shuddering contraption that bore us unsteadily to the 9,200-foot-high Nepalese village of Lukla, where we would begin our trek to Everest itself.

It takes about a week to walk through Nepal's rugged Khumbu region from Lukla to Everest Base Camp. This is Sherpa country: high valleys and deep gorges, where the natives, about twenty thousand of them, traditionally have been subsistence farmers and hunter-gatherers.

No more, however. The roadless Khumbu is now tourist country.

In 1996, an estimated 400,000 tourists swarmed across Nepal, many of them through the Khumbu, a motley herd of foreigners with fistfuls of hard currency to buy food and shelter, trinkets and entertainment. By far the most important among these visitors were questers such as myself, the deep-pocketed (by Sherpa standards) foreigners who arrive each year to climb Sagarmatha—"goddess of the sky"—as Everest is known locally.

The practical-minded Sherpa have traded their hoes and hunting tools for backpacks to act as porters for the various expeditions. Today, a Sherpa can earn a couple of thousand dollars or more lugging gear up and down the mountain for a typical two-month climbing expedition. That's more than ten times Nepal's annual per capita income.

The downside, of course, is that the work is arduous and dangerous: Memorial cairns erected along the upper reaches of the narrow trail to Everest remind you that one in three of those who've died on the mountain has been a Sherpa.

In his definitive chronicle of our doomed expedition, *Into Thin Air,* the journalist Jon Krakauer would describe me as "garrulous" on the walk in. That's probably charitable. I could have talked the ears off a rubber rabbit. I was eager to be liked, accepted, a member of the group. Under such circumstances, I typically talk a lot. If someone had thrown a Frisbee, I would have caught it with my teeth to please them.

The long trail, which rises ever upward through the Khumbu, is the important first step toward preparing yourself to withstand high-mountain conditions that no organism of more than single-cell complexity was ever meant to endure. It's a pleasant trek, in any event, or can be if the route isn't choked with trekkers, climbing parties and the Khumbu's ubiquitous yak trains. Every once in a while you come around a turn and there, off in the distance, is this giant rock, nearly six miles high, thrusting its head up above everything around it.

On clear days you can see a steady plume of ice and snow streaming for a mile or so off Everest's summit. This is the mountain's distinctive white banner, highlighted against the cobalt sky, and a signal that the jet stream, with its winds of 150 to 200 miles an hour, is screaming right over Everest, as it does for most of the year. No one tries to reach the top in these conditions.

But at one time in the spring, and once more in the fall, the banner fades. The ferocious winds lift off Everest, offering a brief window of opportunity for you to go up there, try to tag the top and then hope that you get back down alive.

The Khumbu trail leads up out of the valleys past the treeline to the lower stretches of the twelve-mile-long Khumbu Glacier. At an altitude of approximately sixteen thousand feet you encounter the last settlement of any consequence, a pestilential, medieval hellhole known as Lobuje.

One of the ironies of mountain climbing is that in order to achieve the pristine heights, you must inevitably slog through noisome hog wallows such as Lobuje. There is a straightforward explanation for this. Remote settlements like Lobuje were not established with hordes of visitors in mind. Put several hundred humans and the odd herd of yaks together in a primitive hamlet where dried dung soaked in kerosene is the primary fuel, and sanitation a foreign expression, and you get these characteristically foul trailside settlements. In Lobuje, there was the added frisson of knowledge that the hands that piled up the dung also put out your dinner. Our single hope was to get in and out of Lobuje without contracting any major diseases.

The second I saw Lobuje I realized there was no way I was going to patronize any of its facilities for travelers. Lou and I decided instead to pitch a tent. We had to scout for some time to find a spot both free of offal and upwind of the dung fires.

That season there'd been heavy snow on the trail up to Everest Base Camp, about seven miles beyond Lobuje. Yaks still couldn't negotiate the final stretch, meaning that all gear, equipment and food had to be carried the last few miles on human, mostly Sherpa, backs. Even beneath Lobuje the path was steep and deep with snow. At one turn we saw a bloody yak leg sticking straight out of a snowbank. We were told the limb simply had snapped off as the animal had struggled through the snow.

In Lobuje, we received word that one of our Sherpas had fallen 150 feet into a crevasse and broken his leg while scouting trails on the mountain above us. We all spent an extra day in Lobuje while Rob Hall and one of his guides went ahead to help manage the Sherpa's rescue and evacuation.

Everest Base Camp, where you actually *begin* to climb the mountain at 17,600 feet, is higher than all but two points in the United States, both in Alaska. Interestingly, you cannot see the upper part of Mount Everest from Base Camp. As it is, you are huffing and puffing by the time you get there, and you wonder when you finally arrive, exhausted, just how in the world you're ever going to survive. We arrived on April 7.

The camp is essentially a tent town of about three hundred

transient inhabitants mingling with a bunch of yaks on a glacier. Some structures are built partially of stone, and must be rebuilt each spring due to the constant movement of the glacial ice below. Our cook tent, for instance, had stone walls, as did our dining and storage tents. We also had a first-rate latrine, fashioned from stone, with an opening in the back where our wastes could be shoveled out. This was a necessity under a new rule that mandates all human feces eventually must be removed from the mountain.

This rule, of course, applies only to foreigners. The Sherpas were unconstrained by it. In addition, the feces police there to enforce the rule themselves insouciantly retreated behind any convenient boulder when nature called.

Our facility was easily the grandest in camp, and naturally attracted interlopers. In time, unauthorized deposits became such a problem that a plywood sign with a warning note was placed in the front: "YO! Dude! If you are not a member of the New Zealand Everest Expedition *please* do not use this toilet. We are a way serious bunch of shitters, and will have no trouble filling this thing up without your contribution. Thanks." The message was signed "The Big Cheese," and proved an effective deterrent. Jon Krakauer composed the sign on orders from Rob Hall.

Each climber in our group was assigned an individual tent, a rare and welcome bit of privacy in the otherwise highly communal world of mountain climbing. Our other amenities included a solar-powered satellite phone and fax, and access on three or four occasions to an outdoor shower. To wash oneself under the little dribble of warm water was an exquisite pleasure.

My first fax home from Everest: "If you wish to send me a fax," I wrote by hand, "you probably need to wait until after 10:00 P.M. Dallas time. The fax here is a thermal unit, and it is too cold to print before then. We had a long approach to the mountain. . . . Lower down the valley the villages were nice, but as you get closer they become *very* primitive. Several of us got the trots. I was lucky and have remained well. . . . The climbing group is strong, and has nice folks. I think I am on the weak end of the team, but am doing OK. I think of you and the children each day. All my love, Dear."

"Dear Dear," Peach replied in typescript. "Received your fax last night in the 3:30ish A.M. . . . Scooter [our dog] was certain there was a gremlin on the deck, so he sounded his own special alarm regularly. At 5:00 A.M., I finally put him out in the hall."

She went on to inform me that our car had suffered a fender bender; that our son, Beck, a member of his school's fencing team, had advanced to a national fencing tournament; and that our daughter, Meg, had begun taking voice lessons—all events occurring in Dad's absence, as usual. "We miss you," she signed off. "Love & Kisses, Peach."

The quality of the food on a mountain climb is usually a direct function of availability and the willingness of someone to lug it up there for you. Base Camp on Everest, for example, was a busy place and a big market for provisioners. As a result, we enjoyed eggs every morning. But the higher you go and the farther away from civilization you are, the more practical and less palatable the fare becomes.

By the time you get really high (and have just about stopped caring about food altogether), all that you generally consume are simple carbohydrates and the occasional swallow of soup with cookies or crackers.

The major rigor of Base Camp is boredom; you spend a lot of time getting ready to do things, and a lot of time recovering from doing them, and therefore a lot of time doing nothing. Knowing this from previous excursions, I brought along a favorite author, Carl Hiaasen, to help beguile the hours, plus a little book on learning to juggle, a skill I thought would be fun to master. I became a familiar camp figure, fumbling away in front of my tent. Those of us who had trouble keeping the Sherpas' names straight also used the downtime to take Polaroids of them and then memorize their faces.

For entertainment there was a stereo. Each morning after the Sherpas had burned juniper and chanted their Buddhist prayers, Robin Williams roared "Good Morning, Vietnam!" across the camp, blasting us from our sleeping bags. The rest of the day was rock and roll, plus Indian music from the cooking tent.

We had a couple of parties, for which we broke out the beer. Some people ended up dancing on our dining tent's stone table. It wasn't a mosh pit, exactly, but not unlike one. There were also theme-night dinners, when the food and its preparation and everyone's dress were supposed to complement one team member's salient characteristic.

I'd brought with me several pounds of bodybuilding powder, which I consumed daily to help keep my weight up. So at my theme dinner, the crowd showed up looking like drug dealers. For table decoration, someone produced a mirror and did lines of my powder on it.

By far the predominant physical feature of Base Camp is the

great Khumbu Icefall, which begins just a quarter mile away and stretches up the mountain for two miles and almost two thousand vertical feet.

The Icefall is the midsection of the Khumbu Glacier. It starts above Base Camp at a declivity where the glacier pushes itself out over a precipice, creating giant blocks of ice that tumble downward with an ear-splitting roar. These so-called seracs are the size of small office buildings. They can weigh hundreds of tons. Once inside the Icefall, they continue to groan and thunder along. The whole dangerous mess moves downhill at about four feet a day in the summertime.

Back in 1953, when Edmund Hillary's expedition encountered the Khumbu Icefall on its way to the first successful climb of Everest, team members thought up colorful and highly descriptive names for various stretches of the Icefall. These included Hellfire Alley, the Nutcracker, Atom-Bomb Area and Hillary's Horror. In 1996, we chose to call a giant leaning serac at the top of the Icefall the Mousetrap; no one wanted to be the mouse squashed when the highly unstable Mousetrap inevitably slammed shut. It would snuff out more than just your tender spirits.

In Base Camp, the gargantuan collisions register through your feet as well as your ears, creating in the first-time visitor to Mount Everest the unnerving impression that serial earthquakes and train wrecks are occurring simultaneously just outside your tent.

But that's only the noise.

The reason the Khumbu Icefall concerns you in Base Camp is that it stands between you and the summit. You must go up and down the thing at least five times, spend about twenty hours in it, like an ant trapped in the bottom of an ice machine, if you are to successfully climb Everest.

One of the Icefall's more challenging features is the lightweight aluminum ladders you use to negotiate its jumble of slippery, cantilevered walls and deep crevasses. Anchored to the shifting ice, and lashed to one another, the ladders have a makeshift look and feel to them. On your five round-trip circuits of the Khumbu Icefall, you cross approximately seven hundred of these ladder bridges.

Your first traverse is a religious experience, certainly not something you can practice at home. When you pass through the Icefall, you try to do so at first light, so you can see, but before the surrounding hills and ice fields can reflect the high-altitude sun's intense radiation directly onto the Icefall, partially melting and dislocating the ladders' moorings, and also energizing the chockablock seracs, loosening them to tip, slide and crash all the more.

It can get extremely warm around Base Camp on a sunny day in May. A thermometer left out in the afternoon sun by the Hillary expedition reportedly registered a high temperature of about 150 degrees.

Above the Icefall's upper edge, and also hidden from your view, is the gradually sloping valley of the Western Cwm (pronounced *koom*), which rises another two thousand feet toward an immense, jagged amphitheater, anchored on the left by Everest, with 27,890-foot Lhotse in the center and, on the right, the third of the three brute sisters that dominate the high terrain, 25,790-foot Nuptse.

The Cwm (Welsh for "valley") was named in 1921 by George Mallory, who led the first three assaults on Everest, all from the Tibetan side. Mallory, when asked why he wished to climb Everest, quipped famously, "Because it is there." He may also have been the first person to summit Everest. Then again, maybe he wasn't.

On June 8, 1924, the thirty-eight-year-old Mallory and his protégé, Andrew "Sandy" Irvine, twenty-two, were seen by Noel Odell, a member of their team, about nine hundred feet below the summit and climbing strongly. Then Mallory and Irvine were swallowed from view by a cloud, and disappeared with no trace.

Mallory's fate remained a mystery for seventy-five years, until May of 1999, when an American expedition organized specifically to hunt for the famed British climber found his frozen body approximately two thousand feet below the summit, where he apparently had fallen. Whether George Mallory made it to the top before his fatal plunge is an unsettled debate. His altimeter, a monogrammed scarf, some letters and a pocket knife were recovered in 1999, but the Kodak cameras that Mallory and Irvine brought along to record their ascent were not found; nor (yet) was Irvine's body.

A brief note on my own equipment for Everest: I bought new boots for this trip to replace a set I'd purchased seven years before. They were from the same company, allegedly the same size exactly.

I'd never bought the idea that you need to break in new mountaineering boots; either they fit you from the beginning or they don't. My old boots had developed holes you could shine a light through. I didn't think they could withstand one more ex-pedition.

Unfortunately, the new boots rubbed both my shins, which soon were ulcerated. Wounds at high altitude do not heal. I knew I wouldn't recover until I was off the mountain.

One strategy was to keep the boots loose. But no matter what I did, each step was an agony. I had no choice, in the end, but to wrap my shins in bandages, suck it up and learn to live with it. There was no sense in complaining about something I couldn't change.

When you first arrive at Base Camp, you are acutely aware that every motion you make seems to suck the oxygen out of your body. We do not fully understand all the adjustments the human body makes to the stresses of altitude, but we have learned some techniques for acclimatizing ourselves to the high-altitude environment.

If you, the reader, were by some magic instantly transported to the top of Mount Everest, you would have to deal with the medical fact that in the first few minutes you'd be unconscious, and in the next few minutes you'd be dead. Your body simply cannot withstand the enormous physiologic shock of being sud-denly placed in such an oxygen-deprived environment.

What a climber must do, as we did over several weeks, is to start at Base Camp, climb up, and then climb back down again. Rest and repeat. You keep doing this over and over on Everest, always pushing a little higher each time until (you hope) your body begins to acclimatize. You basically say to your body, "I am going to climb this thing, and I'm taking you with me. So get ready."

But you must be patient. Climb too fast and you elevate your risk of high altitude pulmonary edema (HAPE), in which your lungs fill with water and you can die unless you get down the mountain very fast. Even deadlier is high altitude cerebral edema (HACE), which causes the brain to swell. HACE can induce a fatal coma unless you are quickly evacuated.

There's no way to know beforehand if you are susceptible to these medical conditions. Some people develop symptoms at altitudes as low as ten thousand feet. Moreover, veteran climbers who've never encountered either problem can develop HAPE or HACE without warning.

Similarly unpredictable is a much more common menace, hypoxia, caused by reduced supply of oxygen to the brain. In its milder forms, hypoxia induces euphoria and renders the sufferer a little goofy. Severe hypoxia robs you of your judgment and common sense, not a welcome complication at high altitude. Climbers call the condition HAS, High Altitude Stupid.

My wife offers her own cogent acronym, NUTS, as in Nothing Under the Sun would get her up there in the first place.

The techniques of adapting to altitude are of vital importance to your survival, and not necessarily at extreme altitude only. As recently as twenty years ago, high-altitude sickness killed one in fifty trekkers through the Khumbu each year.

Among the very rarest medical emergencies associated with high-altitude climbing is the one that I unwittingly pioneered, one that nearly killed me. Or it may have saved my life. I'm not sure. There's a sound argument for either point of view.

I'll get to that later.

One of the body's most important physiological adaptations to high altitude is the millions and millions of extra oxygen-bearing red blood cells that your bone marrow produces in response to chronic oxygen deprivation. The extra oxygen-carrying capacity is critical. Still, you *thirst* for air when high on the big mountains. Breathing is such hard work that 40 percent of your total energy output is devoted to it. Each day you can blow off an amazing seven liters of water through your lungs alone.

That leaves you constantly dehydrated. Also, you can no longer sleep or eat. Once in the Death Zone, above 25,000 feet, the thought of food becomes repugnant to most people. Even if you can force yourself to chew and swallow something, your body will not digest it. Yet you are burning about twelve thousand calories a day, which means you're consuming your own tissue—about three pounds of muscle a day—in order to stay alive.

One of my enduring images of Rob Hall on Everest is of his marvelously plastic face, with character lines etched into it by a lifetime spent outside. If you made the least hint of a complaint or lament, Rob would squint up, looking like a demented Popeye, and ask, "You're not gonna be one a' them moaners, are ya?" I, of course, would reply, "No, Rob, no! I'm not going to be one of those moaners. No, sir."

Besides Rob, our guides on Everest were Mike Groom, a plumber from Brisbane, Australia, and Andy Harris, thirty-one, a Kiwi like Hall, who was climbing and guiding for the first time on a so-called eight-thousand-meter mountain, of which there are just fourteen in the world. All soar into the troposphere within a few hundred miles of Mount Everest.

Take a look at any high-altitude camp and you'll discover that this kind of mountaineering is not a beautiful-body sport.

In fact, climbers look pretty much like a bunch of homeless crowding around a steam grate. But Andy was the antithesis of this: a big, good-looking, athletic kid, and a certified mountain monster, despite his lack of experience on the biggest hills.

Then you get down to the grunts, my level. There we find my fellow climber and teammate, forty-two-year-old Jon Krakauer.

I've already mentioned Yasuko Namba, who on this outing would become the oldest woman ever to summit Everest, and the second Japanese woman to do so. By making it to the top that day, Yasuko also would complete the Seven Summits Quest. For these distinctions she would pay an enormous price.

So would Doug Hansen, a forty-six-year-old postal worker from Seattle. Doug had climbed to within three hundred vertical feet of the summit the previous year before being forced to turn back. This year, he was determined, at all costs, to summit Everest.

Rounding out the cast of characters was the baby of our grunt group, Stuart Hutchison, a thirty-five-year-old Canadian cardiologist, and Frank Fischbeck, fifty-three, a Hong Kong publisher of fine books and a gentleman of the old school. Frank provided a measure of civility and dignity to our otherwise pretty raucous group.

Probably everyone's favorite member of our team was Dr. John Taske, fifty-six, an anesthesiologist and Aussie, like Mike Groom. Sharp-witted, with an open and engaging manner, John was a career army officer. Unlike most military physicians, he loved the tougher parts of army life. Nothing made him happier than an underwater demolition school or hazardous duty of any sort. He even earned a British SAS beret, when detached to the elite commando group, the first physician ever to do so.

John was as good at taking a joke as making one. Doug

Hansen and I decided early on that John was romantically interested in a yak we called Buttercup. Since yaks were everywhere, it was easy to keep up a running gag about John and the amorous Buttercup. He seemed to enjoy the raw humor almost as much as we did.

The Australian also had flair. One day he emerged from his tent wearing a sombrero and a red-and-white outfit that looked like a striped sock. He looked more like a cartoon character than a climber. The Sherpas nearly fell out of their boots laughing. If you can wear a getup like that, I guarantee that you're pretty sure of yourself in the company of other men.

Once we were all fully acclimated to altitude—just before our final summit push—Taske supervised a Harvard two-step physiology test for our group. We were curious to see how members of the expedition would handle brief periods of intense effort.

In the test, you repeatedly step up and down about two feet for approximately a minute. Your pulse is monitored before, during and after the exertion. I'd always assumed the mark of the well-trained athlete is a nice, low pulse rate that remains relatively low, even under stress, and recovers quickly afterward.

Two of us, Mike Groom and Lou Kasischke, had exactly this pattern. However, other adaptations seemed to work equally well. Jon Krakauer's resting pulse was approximately 110. Under stress, it promptly plummeted to about 60, then rose back up to maybe 140. When the stepping stopped, it dropped back to 60 and rose right back to 110.

I had a resting pulse of about 90. When stressed, my pulse went straight up to 170 or 180 and stayed there. Soon as I stopped the two-step, it dropped to 60, and then came right back to 90.

I'm told that this pattern of response is similar to that seen among the Sherpas. Clearly a great deal remains to be learned about how we react to stress at high altitude.

The other team to figure large in the May 10 catastrophe was headed by Scott Fischer, a charismatic, ponytailed free spirit from Seattle who ran a high-mountain guide service called Mountain Madness. That pretty much summed up Scott's idea of how you climb a mountain.

He was backed up by Neal Beidleman, who was not normally a guide but an aerospace engineer, as well as by Anatoli Boukreev, a Russian and one of the world's premier high-altitude climbers.

In the Mountain Madness grunt section there was glamour, New York City socialite and celebrity journalist Sandy Hill Pittman. She appeared in climbing gear in *Vogue* before jetting off to Mount Everest, and filed Internet dispatches to NBC as we climbed the mountain. She may have gone to Everest that year in search of fame, but all that Sandy would achieve was notoriety.

When Sandy got back to New York, the media turned on her, portraying her as shallow, without character. That's unfair. Sandy was a strong and determined climber, and a fairly engaging teammate. She was not the cause of our calamity; the storm was.

There also was Tim Madsen, of the Colorado ski patrol, and the object of his affection (as well as one of my favorite people), Charlotte Fox, a handsome gal who gives lie to the idea that high-altitude mountaineering is strictly a male-dominated, adrenaline-driven, macho sport.

I'd climbed with Charlotte in Antarctica and very much admired her, in part because I knew she could outclimb and outmacho me on the best day of my life.

Another fax home: "We have returned to Base Camp for 3 days of food & rest. . . . I remain well and have had only a minor dry cough, but no infections or GI problems. . . . I am convinced that Rob Hall's attention to safety & detail is the best on the mountain. . . . I miss you terribly. All my love, Dear."

"It was good to know you had a nice adventure up on the mountain with the rest of the kids," Peach typed in reply. She reported that Beck (we call him Bub) had a virus, which threatened his appearance at the fencing tournament in Kansas City. Meg's room was being redecorated. Missy, our other dog, had peed all over the paper the painters had put on the floor. "Take care," she closed. "Love and kisses, Peach."

My final fax: "We go up the mountain day after tomorrow. I have the time to receive a fax from you tomorrow. Please drop me a line. It would also be nice if Bub and Meg could enclose a small note. . . . All my love, Dear."

Bub politely declined my invitation to drop a note, but the Weathers women didn't.

Peach: "I'm glad you're having an adventure, and I hope your ailments are minimal. The plumber is here. The condensate drain on the air-conditioning unit is plugged. . . . Much love, Dear."

Meg: "Dadoo. How are we? I'm better now. . . . We performed

today for Mrs. Porter's aunt's birthday. She was 90 years old. For this and my piano recital I was shaking like Missy does when she goes to the vet. . . . I got my hair chopped off up to my shoulder (when wet) and about a little below my ears when dry. . . . Mom says, 'Dinner!' Have to be off, Love, Meg."

Three

Our climb began in earnest on May 9. By then we'd successfully negotiated the Khumbu Icefall, surmounted the Western Cwm, and now were halfway up a moderately steep, four-thousand-foot wall of blue ice called the Lhotse Face, which the prudent climber will traverse very carefully.

This extreme care is a function of the physics involved. With hard ice such as that found on the Lhotse Face, there is no coefficient of friction; you are traction free. Fall into an uncontrolled slide, and your chances of stopping are nil. You're history. A Taiwanese climber named Chen Yu-Nan would discover the truth of this, to his horror, on the morning of May 9.

Because the Lhotse Face is a slope, you pitch Camp Three by carving out a little ice platform for your tent, which you crawl into exhausted, desperate for some rest. No matter how tired you are, however, you must remember a couple of fairly simple rules.

One, don't sleepwalk. Two, when you get up in the morning,

the very first thing you've *got* to do, *without* fail, is put those twelve knives on each climbing boot, your crampons, because they are what stick you down to that hill.

Chen Yu-Nan forgot. He got out of his tent wearing his inner boots, took two steps, and went *zhooooooooop!* down into a crevasse, leading to his death.

Our plan was simple. We were going to get up with the sun and climb all day to get to High Camp on the South Col late that afternoon. We would then rest for three or four hours, get up again and climb all night and through the next day to hit Everest's summit by noon on May 10, and *absolutely* no later than two o'clock.

This point had been drilled into us over the preceding week: *Absolutely no later than two.* If you're not moving fast enough to get to the summit by two, you're not moving fast enough to get back down before darkness traps you on the mountain.

We reached High Camp on schedule late that afternoon. The South Col (from the Latin *collum,* or "neck") is part of the ridge that forms Everest's southeast shoulder and sits astride the great Himalayan mountain divide between Nepal and Tibet. Four groups—too many people, as it turned out—would be bivouacked there in preparation for the final assault: us, Scott Fischer's expedition, a Taiwanese group and a team of South Africans who would not make the summit attempt that night. Altogether, maybe a dozen tents were set up, surrounded by a litter of spent oxygen canisters, the occasional frozen body and the tattered remnants of previous climbing camps.

If you wander too close to the South Col's north rim, you'll tumble seven thousand uninterrupted feet down Everest's Kangshung Face into the People's Republic of China. Make a similar misstep on the opposite side, and you zip to a crash landing approximately four thousand feet down the Lhotse Face.

The wind was blowing quite hard when we crawled into High Camp. It was cold. And at some visceral level I was secretly grateful because I knew that we couldn't climb in those conditions. I was pretty hammered. I said to myself, If you can just rest tonight, you are bound to feel better tomorrow than you feel right now.

This was rank self-deception. The whole point is to arrive at High Camp with just enough energy to get to the summit and then retreat in one piece. I wasn't going to get any stronger up there. Quite the opposite. They call it the Death Zone, because above 25,000 feet, the mountain slowly kills you, whether or not you ever leave your tent.

So we turned in. Doug Hansen, Lou Kasischke, Andy Harris and I all lay under the tent in our sleeping bags, listening to the wind howl. Then about ten that night, the gale quite suddenly blew itself out. A perfect, albeit frigid, calm came over the Death Zone.

"Guys," Rob said, sticking his neck into our tent. "Saddle up! We're going for it!"

I started pulling my gear together, thinking to myself, Well, maybe you've timed this okay. Yeah, you feel pretty crummy. But you feel better than you *thought* you were going to feel.

But I was very concerned (prophetically so) for two members of our group. In the sleeping bag to my immediate left was Doug Hansen. Doug had been sick and wasn't climbing well. He looked like he'd been worked over with an ice ax. Even more so than the rest of us, he hadn't been feeding and watering and resting the machine that has to carry you up the hill.

Being turned around the year before, so close to the top, had come to possess him, to rule his every waking thought. Doug came back to Everest in 1996 vowing that under no circumstance was he going to be turned around again.

I, too, was fanatical about mountain climbing, but I wasn't crazy in *that* way. I lived by mountaineering's general rule that going to any summit is optional. Getting back down is mandatory.

Also, I was like the great majority of climbers in that the only competition I felt was with myself. Before arrival in Nepal, I had set as my personal goal to get at least as far as the South Col. I'd accomplished that. If I didn't make it to the top this time, I'd still feel the trip was worthwhile. Before leaving Dallas I'd told my colleagues that I simply wanted to experience Everest and all it had to offer. I'd probably rephrase that sentiment today.

One of the things that you must honestly ask yourself on a mountain—it is a moral obligation to your fellow climbers—is, With this step, how much do I have left? Can I still turn around and get back down to safety?

I didn't think Doug knew that any longer, and I didn't think he cared.

The other person for whom I was concerned was Yasuko. She was an itty-bitty waif of a person, could not have weighed more than ninety pounds dripping wet. But the gear she had to carry weighed exactly the same as mine and everyone else's. I just didn't think that tiny body of hers could cash the checks that Yasuko's mind was writing.

We got out of the tents and put on our oxygen masks—MIG fighter-pilot surplus. Now we looked like a bunch of homeless top guns on Halloween. We also pulled on our enormous down suits, the kind of thing your mom sent you out in to play in the snow. You can't do much more than waddle in them.

Our group started out first. The Mountain Madness climbers and the Taiwanese were about an hour behind us. It was an exquisite evening as we began to move across the flat expanse of the South Col leading to the summit face. The moon peeked at us over the 27,790-foot summit of Makalu in the distance. The wind was absolutely still. The temperature was about ten below zero, which is quite warm for a big mountain.

Besides our headlamps, there was no artificial light anywhere, which allowed the stars above us to shine with incredible brilliance. You even could see them reflected in that cold blue ice beneath your feet. They seemed so close, as if you could just reach up and pluck them from the heavens, one at a time, put them in your pocket and save them for later.

Our pace was that slow, rhythmic, metronome-like gait ingrained in the frame of my being through years of prior climbing. With each step those knives bite into the ice with a distinctive *creech-ch-ch*. As you move and shift your weight in the cold, the metal in your boots and the bindings on your pack squeak in response.

We moved across the South Col, heading to the summit face. There was nothing to it, really. Just keep plowing straight up. You travel in a private bubble of light from your headlamp, the rest of the world as lost to you as if you were alone on the face of the moon. All you have to do is step and rest, step and rest—

hour after hour after endless hour—until halfway up the face
we shifted over in a traverse to the left.

A traverse is an inherently more dangerous kind of move in
mountaineering. It is harder to protect a traverse. You've got to
be able to see where you're putting your feet. And that spelled a
private disaster for me.

As we started up the summit face, I was fourth in line, following Ang Dorje, our chief climbing Sherpa, Mike Groom and
Jon Krakauer. Over the preceding weeks I'd tried to conserve
my strength. The philosophy is to start slow and back off, because you know it is not how strong you are on day one that
counts. As a result, I had strength in reserve as we moved up.

But I gradually realized, to my deep annoyance, that I
couldn't see the face of this mountain at all, and the reason I
couldn't also slowly dawned on me. I am nearsighted and struggled for years on various mountains with iced-over lenses, balky
contacts and all sorts of gadgets designed to keep my field of vision clear. Nothing worked. So a year and a half before I went
to Mount Everest, I had my eyes operated on so that I would be
safer in the mountains.

The operation was a radial keratotomy, in which tiny inci-
sions are made in one's corneas to alter the eyes' focal lengths
and (presumably) improve vision. However, unbeknownst to
me and to virtually every ophthalmologist in the world, at high
altitude a cornea thus altered will both flatten and thicken,
shortening your focal length and rendering you effectively
blind. That is what happened to me about fifteen hundred feet
above High Camp in the early morning hours of May 10, 1996.

At first I wasn't really worried. I'd experienced minor problems with vision shifts in the past, most recently at Base Camp and when we went through the Icefall. I'd had more than my usual difficulty seeing at night, as well as in the morning until the sun was out enough to require sunglasses.

I felt more inconvenienced than handicapped by the problem and did not mention it to anyone. Nor did I panic when the shift recurred in the dark at 27,500 feet. I really couldn't see, but I knew coming to me in the next couple of hours would be a solution to this difficulty—daylight.

The sun at that altitude is an enormous ball of light so powerful that it can burn the inside of your mouth and the inside of your nose. If you take off those protective glasses, within ten minutes your retinas will be seared to total blindness.

Hence, I expected that, once the sun was fully out, even behind my jet-black lenses my pupils would clamp down to pinpoints and everything would be infinitely focused. I was certain I was right. It had to work.

In the predawn darkness, however, I was too blind to climb. So I stepped out of line and let everyone pass, going from fourth out of thirty-some climbers to absolutely dead last. It wasn't unpleasant, really, watching everybody traipse past me. I basically stood there chatting and acting like a Wal-Mart greeter until the sun began to illuminate the summit face.

As I expected, my vision did begin to clear, and I was able to dig in the front knives on my boots, move across, and head on up to the summit ridge. Then I compounded my problem by reaching to wipe my face with an ice-crusted glove. A crystal painfully lacerated my right cornea, leaving that eye completely blurred. That meant I had no depth perception, and that's not good in that environment. My left eye was a little blurry but basically okay. But I knew that I could not climb above this point, a living-room size promontory called the Balcony, about fifteen hundred feet below the summit, unless my vision improved.

Still believing it would, I said to Rob, "You guys go ahead and boogie on up the hill. At a point that I can see, I'll just wander up after you."

It was about 7:30 A.M.

"Beck," he answered in that unmistakable Kiwi accent, "I don't like that idea. You've got thirty minutes. If you can see in thirty minutes, climb on. If you cannot see in thirty minutes, I don't want you climbing."

"Okay." I hesitated. "I'll accept that." This was not a willing and happy answer; I had come too far to quit so close to the summit. But I also recognized the common sense in what Hall said.

Then I did something really stupid.

"You know," I continued, "if I *can't* see in that thirty-minute window you've given me, as soon as I can see I'm just going to head back down to the High Camp."

Hall said no to that notion, too.

"I don't like that idea any better than your last one," he said. "If I come down off the top of this thing and you're not standing here, I'm not going to have any idea whether or not you've gone down safely to High Camp, or if you've just gone for an eight-thousand-foot wipper. I want you to promise me—I'm serious about this—I want you to promise me that you're going to stay here until I come back."

I said, "Rob, cross my heart, hope to die, I'm sticking."

It didn't enter my mind that he might never come back.

I waited through the morning. It was a beautiful day. A cloudless sky. The wind was still. This enormous cathedral of mountains stretching as far as my good eye could see. The curvature of the earth was visible beneath my feet.

By noon, three climbers from our group descended toward me: Stuart Hutchison, Lou Kasischke and John Taske (Frank Fischbeck already had turned back). They said there was a slowdown at the uppermost part of the mountain at Hillary Step, a natural obstacle on the ridge leading directly to the summit. Because of the bottleneck of climbers, the three of them realized there was no way they could make the summit by two.

So Stuart, Lou and John decided to come down, and as they came by me, standing alone, getting colder and colder on the Balcony, they said, "Well, come on down with us."

"Uh, I've really put myself in a box here," I answered. "I've promised Hall I will stay put. We have no radio, so I have no way to tell him that I'm leaving. It would be as if I never honored that commitment at all. I just don't think I can do that now."

They said good-bye and continued on down. Three wise men. In retrospect I clearly should have joined them. But I didn't then sense I was in any imminent danger. It was a perfect day. Also, even though I knew that I was not going to climb the mountain that day, I still hated to give up. To go down with them would be to absolutely concede I'd failed.

Lou Kasischke, by the way, made it back to camp safely, but would endure his own special horror there. Recall that in High Camp Lou shared a tent with me, Doug Hansen and Andy Harris. During the summit assault, Lou removed his protective glasses for too long, and consequently went snow-blind. As the storm came in that evening, he would lie there alone, unseeing, listening to the wind trying to tear the tent apart, wondering what had happened to his three tent mates.

Four

I expected Rob no later than three. The hour came and went, as did four and five. Now I began to worry. The sun was my great ally, but the shadows were beginning to lengthen as it started to set. With it, those pinpoint irises of mine would begin to open up and I'd be blind again—soon.

I could sense the mountain starting to put itself to bed. The light went flat. It began to get a little colder. The wind picked up. The snow began to move, and I realized I'd stayed too long at the party. I was trapped.

I was beginning to lose it. Although I'd been breathing bottled oxygen and was not hypoxic, I had been standing or sitting for ten hours without moving much. The cold was beginning to act like an anesthetic on my mind. I hallucinated seeing people. They drifted in and out of focus.

I recognize now that I was sinking, cold past shivering, overtaken by a calm apathy, unable to appreciate my peril. The water bottles inside my jacket against the skin of my chest had frozen solid. If I'd been left there, I probably would have slowly frozen to death, without even trying to stir.

Then Jon Krakauer came along and I collected myself. He was plainly exhausted. We spoke for a bit. Jon said that Rob was still up there on the ridge, at least three hours behind him, which meant that all deals were off. There was no way I could wait three more hours. On the other hand, there also was no way now for me to descend unassisted.

Krakauer did the right thing. Although our guide Mike Groom was just twenty minutes behind him on the trail, he offered to help me down. I, in turn, was uncomfortable with inflicting myself on Jon. I declined with thanks, saying I'd wait for Groom. I think Jon heaved a little sigh of gratitude.

Another half hour or so passed, and here came Mike Groom with Yasuko. She looked like a walking corpse, so exhausted she could barely stand. Fortunately, Neal Beidleman and some other members of the Fischer group also came along just then, including Sandy Pittman, Charlotte Fox and Tim Madsen, all of whom had summitted, and all of whom were close to the limits of their endurance.

Yasuko and I were the acute problems, however. Neal took her and headed on down the Triangle. Mike short-roped me, which is exactly what it sounds like. One end of a rope went around the waist of the downhill climber, me. Twenty feet back was Mike, who'd use muscle and leverage to stabilize me as we descended.

It was nearly 6:00 P.M. by now.

Climbing down a mountain is a lot more dangerous than climbing up. If you're going to get yourself killed, that's generally when it happens. In this case, we had the added problem of exhaustion and blindness and one other little detail, my crampons. They were so-called switchblade crampons, good for technical climbing but prone to clog up in wet or sticky snow. Pretty quickly, the accumulated snow extends down beneath the blade tips and suddenly you're better equipped for skiing than clinging to the mountainside.

So here goes. I move, commit and plant my weight on what I believe to be that hill. Wrong. I step onto nothing but air and come whipping off the front of the face. The rope snaps taut, and pulls Mike right off his feet.

Both of us start to slide. We take our ice axes, jam them into the hill, and both of us roll our body weight on top of them to stop the fall.

We do this another two or three times before we get all the way down. Mike later described the experience as "somewhat unnerving." Little did he guess what lay dead ahead.

Except for some rips in my down suit and a whole lot of wounded pride, I was fine, and heartily relieved. We were back on the South Col—practically home free. In less than an hour of easy traverse we were going to be in those tents, in those sleeping bags, drinking hot tea and putting the long, exhausting day to bed.

But as we all began to move, we heard that throaty rumble come surging up the mountain. Suddenly, the blizzard detonated all around us. It crescendoed into a deafening roar. A thick wall of clouds boiled across the South Col, wrapping us in white, blotting out every discernible feature until the only visible objects were our headlamps, which seemed to float in the maelstrom. Neal Beidleman later said it was like being lost in a bottle of milk.

It quickly became *incredibly* cold.

I grabbed Mike's sleeve. He was my eyes. I dared not lose contact with him.

We instinctively herded together; nobody wanted to get separated from the others as we groped along, trying to get the feel of the South Col's slope, hoping for some sign of camp. We turned one way, and that wasn't it. We turned again, and that wasn't it. In the space of a few minutes, we lost all sense of direction; we had no idea where we were facing in the swirling wind and noise and cold and blowing ice.

We continued to move as a group, until suddenly the hair stood up on the back of Neal's neck. Experience and intuition told Beidleman that mortal danger lurked nearby.

"Something is wrong here," he shouted above the din. "We're stopping." It was a good decision. We were not twenty-five feet from the seven-thousand-foot vertical plunge off the Kangshung Face. From where we stopped the ice sloped away at a steep angle. A few more paces and the whole group would have just skidded off the mountain.

When we stopped something else stopped, too—that internal furnace that keeps you alive. The only way to stay warm in those conditions is through constant activity. To stand still is to freeze to death, which already was happening to me.

I could no longer feel or move my right hand, no surprise under the circumstances, and normally a fairly simple problem to fix. You take off two of the three gloves you wear and jam the affected hand beneath your coat against your bare chest. When it's warmed sufficiently, you take it back out, put on the gloves and go about your business.

Now, I had been in very cold places, but what happened next was a complete shock. When I pulled those two outer gloves off, the skin on my hand and my arm immediately froze solid, even underneath that third expedition-weight glove. The shooting pain of instant frostbite so startled me that I lost my grip on the glove in my left hand, which the wind grabbed—*whoooooosh*—and sent into outer space.

There was another pair of gloves in the pack on my back. But they might as well have been under my bed at home. In such a storm, there was no way I could take off that pack, put it down and rummage through it. The wind was strong enough to lift me bodily off the ground and drop me, which at one point it did.

I didn't have the time, or presence of mind, to consider my exposed right hand and forearm's probable fate, or how I might fare in the future as a one-handed pathologist. I did reinsert my hand under my coat, a frozen Napoleon.

Life and death were now the issue for all of us, with the odds against the former lengthening each moment.

Just then, however, the racing clouds opened briefly above us, revealing the Big Dipper. I remember Klev Schoening, one of the Mountain Madness clients, calling out, "I've seen the stars. I know where the camp is!"

Hope.

We rapidly formulated a plan. The strongest among us—including Beidleman and Schoening—would make a high-speed trek in the direction of camp. If Schoening had his directions straight, and if they found the blue tents of High Camp, they'd get help and rescue the rest of us.

If they didn't make it, we were history anyway.

Mike Groom and I discussed the situation. I could still walk okay, but because I couldn't see, I'd have to hold on to his arm, which would slow him down. Since my life now depended on someone getting to camp and back before I froze to death, I agreed to stay.

There was no question about Charlotte, Sandy and Yasuko. None of them could walk without help. So we four would remain. As the others moved away, Tim Madsen stopped abruptly.

"I am not going to leave Charlotte here," he said. "You guys can go, but I'm not going to leave her."

That took a lot of guts. Unspoken among us was the reasonable expectation that the women and I—and now Tim—were dead meat. Here's to the power of love.

As Beidleman, Groom and Schoening lurched off into the storm, Yasuko silently, desperately clung to Neal's arm. Soon her hand slipped away, and they were gone. Then she and the rest of us dropped down to the ice and arranged ourselves like a dog pack, back to back and belly to belly, hoping to conserve heat, trying to get out of that wind.

Charlotte Fox:

I remember Beck saying to me at that point, "Well, Charlotte, this is the darnedest thing in the world, isn't?" Uh-huh. You got that one right, Beck.

Sleep was our deadliest enemy. Every mountaineer knows that if you allow yourself to be taken down by that cold, it is a one-way ticket to death. There are no exceptions. Your core temperature plunges until your heart stops. So we yelled at each other, and hit each other and kicked each other. Anything to remain awake.

Charlotte cried out, "I don't care anymore! All I want to do is die quickly!"

"Uh-huh!" Tim told her. "Wrong answer, Charlotte. Move your legs! Move your hands. C'mon!"

Charlotte Fox:

I was freezing to death. It was so painful, I just wanted it to be over.

Sandy Pittman fell apart.

"I don't want to die!" she yelled. "I don't want to die! My face is freezing! My hands are freezing! I don't want to die!"

I said nothing, in part because Sandy was covering it pretty well. She certainly was expressing my point of view.

(Sandy later told me that in the midst of the freezing horror, she'd had this odd dream of being at peace in a tea garden. For some reason, I was playing a flute in this reverie. I appreciated being included. In fact, it reminded me that at one point in my life, I'd intended to take up the flute. Maybe in my next life.)

From about the time of Sandy's screams until the next day, my memory is vague or nonexistent. I was starting to freeze, which was not unpleasant. You really do start feeling warmer. Then I had a sense of floating. I wondered if someone was dragging me across the ice. I wasn't really well enough glued together to comprehend these sensations.

Charlotte Fox:

It was so windy that I had my hood pulled tightly around my face. I wasn't really looking around. But Tim remembers Beck standing up on a rock, putting his arms out and saying, "Okay, I've got this all figured out." Then he toppled over and that's the last Tim saw of him.

Five

Neal, Mike and Klev somehow did find High Camp that night, but were on their hands and knees by the time they did. None of them had anything left. They weren't going to return for us; they couldn't. The Sherpas in camp wouldn't. There was no one else to try, except for the Russian, Anatoli Boukreev.

That day, Anatoli had forsaken his duty as a guide. While everyone was struggling up and down the ridge to the summit, or stacked up like cordwood at the Hillary Step, Anatoli climbed for himself, by himself, without oxygen. He just went straight up, tagged the summit, and came straight back down. Because he lacked oxygen, he couldn't persist in the cold, and was forced to retreat to the shelter of his tent.

So Boukreev had been in his tent recovering for hours, and if that was where his story had ended that night, the climbing community would have stripped the flesh right off his bones. They are not a forgiving bunch.

But Anatoli did what no one else could, or would do. He

went out into that storm three times, searching both for Scott Fischer, who froze to death on the mountain, about twelve hundred feet above the South Col, and for us. Boukreev twice was driven back to camp by the wind and cold. The third time he located our little huddle by the face and brought in each of the three Fischer climbers—Tim, Charlotte and Sandy. He left behind Yasuko and me, the Hall climbers.

Charlotte Fox:

I just remember Anatoli suddenly being there. He grabbed me first. I stood up and walked in with him. He led me by the hand. Then he brought in Sandy and Tim. I don't recall any conversation about Beck and Yasuko.

Anatoli later told at least three stories of what occurred out there on the South Col. It doesn't matter which one was true. In that moment, by saving those three people who otherwise surely would have died, Anatoli Boukreev became a hero.

Let that be the way Anatoli is remembered. On Christmas Day of 1997, Boukreev was killed in an avalanche on Annapurna.

Which brings me to the rest of the lost climbers from my group: Rob Hall, Doug Hansen and Andy Harris.

Doug Hansen, as I said, was climbing poorly. The year before, when he'd come so close to that summit, Doug had looked good going up. But when he turned around, he lost it and had to be helped down.

Your body doesn't carry you up there. Your mind does. Your

body is exhausted hours before you reach the top; it is only through will and focus and drive that you continue to move. If you lose that focus, your body is a dead, worthless thing beneath you.

Doug kept climbing past two o'clock, then three o'clock and four o'clock, ignoring the risk. I don't know why Rob let him do it. But when Doug finally reached all the way to the summit, it was a rerun of 1995. That's all he brought with him. That's all he had.

Now Rob Hall had a heck of a problem on his hands. He could not save Doug. He could not rescue him. Doug had to get down on his own legs.

Rob called down to Base Camp. He was told, "Rob, this is hard, but you have *got* to leave him. You cannot save him. Save yourself."

It comes as no surprise to those of us who knew him that Rob could never do that, leave Doug alone on the mountain to save himself. If he did, Rob could never again look in the mirror.

So this father-to-be would damn himself if he did not, and be doomed if he did. He got back on the radio and said, "We're in desperate trouble," and asked for help. Young Andy Harris, who was about a third of the way down to High Camp and pretty much exhausted himself, heard this.

Andy, sapped by his exertions as well as an intestinal bug he contracted in Lobuje, turned and slowly labored his way back up that hill. He reached an oxygen cache and took several canisters all the way back to Doug and Rob near the summit. What happened next is unclear. However, hours passed as they tried to get Doug across the knife-edged summit ridge.

Rob and Andy made it to the South Summit, but Doug did

not. He apparently fell on the way. Andy stayed with Rob until sometime in the night when, disoriented and physically spent, he disappeared into the storm, never to be found.

Harris's ice ax later was recovered near Rob's body, suggesting that Andy had reached his limit. No climber readily surrenders his ice ax.

Rob lived through that night, but late the next afternoon, as darkness began to fall, when there was no longer any hope of a rescue, Base Camp called his wife, Jan, in New Zealand and patched her through to her dying husband. Everyone on that mountain with a radio bore silent witness to their last moments together. Hall had regained his faculties. He and Jan decided at that moment to name their unborn child Sarah.

Jan to Rob: "Don't feel that you're alone. I'm sending all my positive energy your way."

Rob to Jan: "I love you. Sleep well, my sweetheart. Please don't worry too much."

Both of them knew exactly what lay ahead. When those moments had passed and Rob no longer had to be strong, you could hear him quietly weeping as he faced his own death. He didn't know the radio was still on.

Six

The storm relented on the morning of the eleventh. The winds dropped to about thirty knots. Stuart Hutchison and three Sherpas went in search of Yasuko and me. They found us lying next to each other, largely buried in snow and ice.

First to Yasuko. Hutchison reached down and pulled her up by her coat. She had a three-inch-thick layer of ice across her face, a mask that he peeled back. Her skin was porcelain. Her eyes were dilated. But she was still breathing.

He moved to me, pulled me up, and cleaned the ice out of my eyes and off my beard so he could look into my face. I, like Yasuko, was barely clinging to life. Hutchison would later say he had never seen a human being so close to death and still breathing. Coming from a cardiologist, I'll accept that at face value.

What do you do? The superstitious Sherpas, uneasy around the dead and dying, were hesitant to approach us. But Hutchison didn't really need a second opinion here. The answer was, you leave them. Every mountaineer knows that once you go into hypothermic coma in the high mountains, you never, ever wake up. Yasuko and I were going to die anyway. It would only endanger more lives to bring us back.

I don't begrudge that decision for my own sake. But how much strain would be entailed in carrying Yasuko back? She was so tiny. At least she could have died in the tent, surrounded by people, and not alone on that ice.

Hutchison and the Sherpas got back to camp and told everyone that we were dead. They called down to Base Camp, which notified Rob's office in Christchurch, which relayed the news to Dallas. On a warm, sunny Saturday morning the phone rang in our house. Peach answered and was told by Madeleine David, office manager for Hall's company, Adventure Consultants, that I had been killed descending from the summit ridge.

"Is there any hope?" Peach asked.

"No," David replied. "There's been a positive body identification. I'm sorry."

About four in the afternoon, Everest time—twenty-two hours into the storm—the miracle occurred: I opened my eyes. Several improbable, if not impossible, events would follow in succession. I would stand and struggle alone back to High Camp. Next day I'd stand again and negotiate the Lhotse Face. Then there would be the highest-altitude helicopter rescue ever. Those were the *big* things. The miracle was a quiet thing: I opened my eyes and was given a chance to try.

In my confused state, I at first believed that I was warm and comfortable in my bed at home, with Texas sunlight streaming in through the window. But as my head cleared I saw my glove-less hand directly in front of my face, a gray and lifeless thing.

I smashed it onto the ice. It bounced, making a sound like a block of wood. This had the marvelous effect of focusing my attention: I am not in my own bed. I am somewhere on the mountain—I don't know where. I can't see at any distance, but I know that I am alone.

It would take a while to recapture the previous night in my mind. When I did, I assumed the others all were rescued and that for some reason I was overlooked, left behind. Was it something I said?

Innately, I knew that the cavalry was not coming. If they were going to be there, they already would have been there. I was on my own.

One mystery still unsolved is why I no longer was lying next to Yasuko. She remained where Stuart Hutchison and the Sherpas found, and left, us that morning. But I awoke from the coma alone and a good distance away that afternoon. I can only surmise that sometime between morning and late day I semi-revived and somehow made my way (perhaps fifty yards) in the direction of High Camp before collapsing again.

Somewhere in the midst of all this came another shock—my epiphany. Suddenly, my family appeared in my mind's eye—Peach, Bub and Meg. This was not a group portrait or some remembered photo. My subconscious summoned them into vivid focus, as if they might at any moment speak to me. I knew at that instant, with absolute clarity, that if I did not stand at once, I would spend an eternity on that spot.

I thought I was inured to the idea of dying on the mountain. Such a death may even have seemed to me to have a romantic and noble quality. But even though I was prepared to die, I just wasn't ready.

I struggled to my feet and took off my pack, discarding it

along with the ice ax. This was going to be a one-shot deal. If I don't make that camp, I'm not going to need equipment, I decided. It would just slow me down. For a fleeting moment I reflected that these likely were my last earthly possessions.

I also realized at just that moment that I had to take a major-league leak. There was no choice but to let fly in my suit. At least that warmed me up, temporarily.

My first idea was to walk in a sort of grid. I started out in a succession of squares, searching for some landmark or way to orient myself. Soon, however, I realized that was getting me nowhere.

Then I recollected that the night before someone had yelled out during the storm, "What direction does the wind blow over High Camp?"

The answer was "It blows up that face, across the camp, across the Col." Which meant that if the wind had not shifted, High Camp ought to be somewhere upwind.

So I chose that direction, feeling it was as good as any of the 359 other choices I had. If I fell down, I was determined to get up. If I fell down again, I would get up again. And I was going to keep moving until I fell down and could not stand or I walked into that camp, or I walked off the face of the mountain.

Both my hands were completely frozen. My face was destroyed by the cold. I was profoundly hypothermic. I had not eaten in three days, or taken water for two days. I was lost and I was almost completely blind.

You cannot sweat that small stuff, I said to myself. You have to *focus* on that which must be done, and do that thing.

I began to move in that same repetitive, energy-conserving

motion that my body knows so well. The ground was uneven, scattered with little ledges maybe five to eight inches deep that in the flat light of late afternoon were invisible to me.

Each time I encountered one of these hidden ledges, I would fall. At first, I instinctively put out my hands to break the fall, but I didn't want to compound the effects of the frostbite by further damaging my hands, so I held them close to my body and tried to turn on my back, or on my side, each time I slipped and fell. I hit the frozen ground pretty hard. *Blam!* Each time there'd be this little light show in my head from the jolt. Then I'd get up and start again.

Part of me was apathetic, even accepting, a reprise of the previous afternoon up on the Balcony. The sun was going lower and lower, and I knew the second it was gone, I was gone, too. I'd lose the light, and the temperature would come screaming down. I had thoughts of falling one last time and not being able to get up and then just watching that sun set.

What surprised me about that realization was I was not at all frightened by it. I am not a particularly brave individual, and I would have expected myself to be terrified as I came to grips with that moment. But that was not what I felt at all.

No, I was overwhelmed by an enormous, encompassing sense of melancholy. That I would not say good-bye to my family, that I would never again say "I love you" to my wife, that I would never again hold my children, was just not acceptable.

"Keep moving," I said to myself again and again.

I began to hallucinate again, getting awfully close to losing it. Things were really moving around.

Then I saw these two odd blue rocks in front of me, and I

thought for one moment, Those might be the tents! Just as quickly I said to myself, Don't! When you walk up to them and they are nothing but rocks, you're going to be discouraged and you might stop. *You cannot do that.* You are going to walk right up to them and you are going to walk right past them. It makes *no* difference.

I concentrated on these blue blurs, torn between believing they were camp and fearing they were not, until I got within a hundred feet of them—when suddenly a figure loomed up! It was Todd Burleson, the leader of yet another climbing expedition, who beheld a strange creature lurching toward him in the twilight.

Burleson later shared his first impressions of me with a TV interviewer:

"I couldn't believe what I saw. This man had no face. It was completely black, solid black, like he had a crust over him. His jacket was unzipped down to his waist, full of snow. His right arm was bare and frozen over his head. We could not lower it. His skin looked like marble. White stone. No blood in it."

Seven

Todd Burleson's amazement stemmed in part from my appearance, and in part from the news he'd received that everyone above High Camp, including me, was dead.

He quickly recovered his composure, reached out and took me by the arm to the first tent—the dead Scott Fischer's tent—where they put me into two sleeping bags, shoved hot water bottles under my arms, and gave me a shot of steroids.

"You are *not* going to believe what just walked into camp," they radioed down to Base Camp. The response back was "That is fascinating. But it changes nothing. He is going to die. Do not bring him down."

Fortunately, they didn't tell me that.

Conventional wisdom holds that in hypothermia cases, even so remarkable a resurrection as mine merely delays the inevitable. When they called Peach and told her that I was not as dead as they thought I was—but I was critically injured—they were trying not to give her false hope. What she heard, of course, was an entirely different thing.

I also demurred from the glum consensus. Having reconnected with the mother ship, I now believed I had a chance to actually survive this thing. For whatever reason, I seemed to have tolerated the hypothermia, and genuinely believed myself fully revived. What I did not at first think about was the Khumbu Icefall, which simply cannot be navigated without hands. I was going to require another means of exit, something nobody had ever tried before.

They left me alone in Scott Fischer's tent that night, expecting me to die. On a couple of occasions I heard the others referring to "a dead guy" in the tent. Who could that be? I wondered as I slipped in and out of wakefulness.

To complicate matters, the storm came roaring back, every bit as ferocious as the previous night. It shook that tent and me in it as if we were absolutely weightless. I remembered how Scott had talked about a new tent he was trying out, how it was an experimental, lightweight model, extremely flexible. I wondered if I was in that tent and, if so, how well it had been secured to the ground. The wind certainly was strong enough to blow me and the tent clear off the South Col.

With each gust it pressed so heavily on my chest and face that I couldn't breathe. In the brief moments between the gusts, I rolled onto my side, eventually discovering that if I lay on my side, I could breathe even as the tent pressed down on me.

My right hand and forearm were less than useless in all this. They started to swell and discolor down to my wristwatch. I tried desperately to bite the thing off, but Seiko makes a darn good watchband, and I failed.

All the commotion and discomfort notwithstanding, I must

have lost consciousness repeatedly that night. I don't remember the blizzard blowing out the doors and filling the tent with snow, but it did. I don't remember being blasted out of my sleeping bag, but clearly I was, because that was how I found myself at dawn.

Peach:

I can sort of understand why no one was able or willing to risk their lives to rescue Beck or Yasuko. I even sort of understand the medical edict from Base Camp that Beck should be left to die at High Camp. What I don't understand is why they left him alone in that tent overnight.

I mean, if they were lucid enough to understand a doctor's directive, they should have had the presence of mind not to leave him all alone. They might at least have checked on him a couple of times.

I've thought this over again and again. Where was their basic human compassion? Being in the tent with Beck certainly would not have endangered anyone. If they figured he was going to die, then being there to hear his final words, and perhaps pass them on to those he left behind, would have been a tremendous comfort to us.

Nearly everyone packed up to break camp at daybreak, and they did so very quietly. I didn't hear any of it. Besides myself, only Jon Krakauer, and Todd Burleson and Pete Athans, who were guiding the same expedition together, remained in camp.

I heard a noise outside.

"Hello!" I yelled. "Anybody out there?" Krakauer, who was checking out each tent before he, too, headed down the mountain, stuck his head inside. When he saw me, Jon's jaw dropped right down to the middle of his chest. I was supposed to be dead.

"What the hell does a person have to do around here to get a little service!" I said, then added, "Jon, if you don't mind, would you ask Pete Athans to step over here? I'd really like to talk to him."

Athans, an acquaintance from previous expeditions, looked in and saw that I, in fact, was still alive. I was fully dressed. I had my boots on. (You can't take them off because your feet will swell and you can't get back in them.) So it was a relatively simple thing for me to stand, put my crampons back on with Pete and Todd's help, and drink two liters of tea.

Now the dead guy was ready to head down the Lhotse Face.

I peed down my leg again as I got my glacier glasses on. With Pete in front of me and Todd behind, holding on to my harness, we made it about a quarter way down the face to an area of crumbly rock called the Yellow Band. There we were met by members of an IMAX film crew: Ed Viesturs, America's strongest high-altitude climber, as well as Robert Schauer, an Austrian photographer, who'd escort me the rest of the way down to Camp Three, which is 23,400 feet above sea level.

David Breashears, the IMAX director and cinematographer, joined us there. At that point, all I wanted to do was crawl into a tent and go to sleep, but David said no, we had to keep moving down.

I said, "David, if you believe I can do it, I guess I can."

After a short rest and some more tea, we set off again, this time down a very steep part of the slope to Camp Two on the Western Cwm at 21,300 feet. We were walking so close to each other that I remarked if we were in my home state of Georgia, we'd be married.

David walked in front of me. I rested one arm on the back of his pack. Each time he lifted his foot off the ice, I'd slide my crampons into his print. Behind me, either Ed or Robert kept a grip on my climbing harness. In this way we slowly lurched down the face.

The three of them—David, Ed and Robert—are elite mountaineers, among the most famous and accomplished mountain climbers in the world. It wasn't lost on me that I, the ultimate grunt at the end of his climbing career, suddenly was surrounded by a Dream Team of mountaineering. Another of life's little ironies.

It should be noted that escorting me down the Lhotse Face was among the least of the selfless acts performed by David and the rest of the IMAX team in that emergency. When they heard of the developing tragedy, they called up to High Camp on the South Col and instructed that whoever needed their cached stores there—oxygen, fuel, food, batteries, whatever—had only to cut open their tents and take anything that was needed. These men were acting as members of the brotherhood of the rope, undeterred by the real possibility that giving up their painstakingly cached supplies might scuttle a $7 million venture.

I'm thankful that it did not.

As we descended the Lhotse Face, I asked David whether he'd

mind if we sang a little bit to help me keep up my spirits. I'm sure he thought I was crazy. Nevertheless we soon were singing Aretha Franklin's "Chain of Fools," which seemed entirely appropriate to the moment. Trying to keep everyone's spirits up, I even tried some vaudeville-grade humor.

"They told me this trip was going to cost an arm and a leg," I quipped shamelessly to David. "So far, I've gotten a little better deal."

Our mess tent at Camp Two was turned into a hospital. Inside, Dr. Ken Kamler, a hand surgeon from New York, and a Danish physician, Dr. Henrik Jessen Hansen, were seeing to the walking wounded.

These included Gau Ming-Ho, leader of the Taiwanese expedition, who goes by the nickname "Makalu." He'd also been caught late on the mountain, and had managed to get as far down as Scott Fischer's perch twelve hundred feet above the South Col, where three Sherpas eventually rescued him, leaving the comatose Fischer behind.

At Camp Two they stripped off my gear—including the Seiko—and in the space of a minute or so I was lying naked on the floor. It was a coed crowd, of course, but I could have cared less if they sold tickets.

They eventually put me in a sleeping bag, and my hands in two bowls of warm water to begin thawing them. They were later dressed in silver nitrate, which is also used on burns—it'll kill anything—and heavily bandaged into two big mitts. I took some Advil, a vasodilator and a little soup.

Someone started a saline-solution IV in my right arm. It was very cold at Camp Two. Even though they ran the coils through warm water, when the fluid hit my veins it felt like an icicle in my heart.

This was when I began hearing rumors of a helicopter rescue—Peach's hidden hand. It sounded like a fairy tale: Ain't ever happened. Ain't ever gonna happen. The lowest camp on that mountain was way above the rated ceiling of the helicopter in question, an American EuroCopter Squirrel belonging to the Royal Nepalese Army. The air was so thin and unstable at that altitude that we'd simply fall out of the sky.

However, nobody told Peach about this. And since she didn't know it could not be done, she did it. Assisted by her bunch of North Dallas power moms—any one of whom I believe could run a Fortune 500 company out of her kitchen—they proceeded to call everybody in the United States. If you did not personally receive a phone call from my wife or one of her associates in this effort, it was because you weren't home.

They enlisted my home state senator, Kay Bailey Hutchison, as well as Tom Daschle, the Democratic Senate minority leader, who lit a fire under the State Department, which in turn contacted a fine young man in the embassy in Katmandu, David Schensted, who worked with a beautiful Nepalese woman, Inu K.C. The initials stand for Khatri Chhetri, and they mean Inu is a member of a warrior caste, *the* warrior caste of Nepal.

To be K.C. is a very serious matter. You live according to a much more demanding personal code than others. After several pilots had declined (quite reasonably) to attempt the rescue, Inu told Schensted, "I know a man who believes that he has a brave heart, but he's never been sufficiently challenged to know if this is true. I will ask him."

They found forty-two-year-old Lieutenant Colonel Madan K.C., just as he was taking his second shot on the first hole of the Royal Nepal Golf Club. Rather than refusing such a perilous mission, as any mortal might, Madan K.C. accepted the challenge. "I will do this thing," he said. "I will rescue the Beck."

The optimum, indeed only time to hazard such a risky operation on Everest is early in the morning. As was true with moving through the Khumbu Icefall, the sun complicates high-altitude aviation by heating the atmosphere, making it even thinner and more unstable. Madan wanted it to be as cool and calm as possible.

We got up at five-thirty that morning and moved the two thousand vertical feet down the Cwm to Camp One at the top edge of the Icefall. As we arrived, the radio came alive. A voice announced from Base Camp, "The helicopter is here, and he's going to try it. He's here for Weathers. Get ready. One climber. One climber only."

Madan:

The American embassy alerted us that Beck Weathers was sick on the mountain at twenty thousand feet. We had never been that high before, so we discussed it among ourselves. That is a very, very dangerous place, with high winds. But when I am on duty it is my moral obligation not to back out when I can save someone's life.

I said to the American embassy, "We'll try."

I planned to take off from Katmandu at six o'clock that morning. But when we got to the airport there was a message:

"Very high winds. Don't send the helicopter." Then they called again: "The wind is down. Send the helicopter."

We took off. We were just going to try. We were not confident. We had never been that high before, and you have to fly within feet of the Khumbu Icefall to get up into that valley. Power is almost nil.

You have to be very precise. You are flying at the upper limits of everything.

Just as we received the radio message, a group of Sherpas came running down the valley toward us. They were dragging something, which turned out to be Makalu Gau, whose feet had been destroyed by the cold. He could not stand.

Now we had a problem. We talked about it, and I told the others that I couldn't get on the helicopter and leave Makalu. I think that was the right thing to do, but that wasn't why I said it. I didn't want to second-guess myself every day for the rest of my life.

Then we saw the Squirrel. The shiny green machine rose directly above us, and moved up the valley, ascended toward us and then just disappeared off the face. I thought to myself, This guy is not stupid. This was a supremely dumb idea. If he puts the machine down for *any* reason and cannot take off, he is a dead man. He's *got* to know that.

He was up there in civilian clothes. He was not a climber. He did not have the clothing. He did not have the experience. He did not have the skills. He'd be trapped above the Khumbu Icefall, two thousand of the most vicious feet of real estate on earth. Altitude sickness would kill him before he could walk out of there.

Madan:

We flew up to Camp One, but we didn't see anybody. Usually, with a rescue there's a flag or something like that. So we flew up to Camp Two and then came back down when we saw people pulling a body through the snow. He looked like he was in real trouble.

At that altitude, the helicopter was too heavy for us to attempt the rescue. My copilot said, "Let's go. It is not possible."

I said, "Let me try."

One thing, you have to make up your mind. Either yes or no. If you don't you can make a mistake up there. I was certain— "Okay, I'm going now."

So I flew back down to Base Camp and dropped my copilot and some gear and fuel. Then I came back up alone—I had twenty minutes of fuel—and made a pass by the camp only one foot above the ground. I was looking to see if all the fresh snow would blow up. If it did I could not land. If I had landed and not been able to take off, I wouldn't be alive today. It was fifteen degrees Fahrenheit.

Once again the helicopter rose. One lone man. He moved up that valley with deliberate and delicate precision, and lay those skids down on the surface. He dared not let the weight of the helicopter descend. He had no idea if this was solid, or if this was chiffon over air. You never know up there whether you're standing above a crevasse.

The power was full on. His hands were frozen on the controls. His head didn't move left or right—that changes your depth perception. We grabbed Makalu like a sack of potatoes, ran him over there and threw him in the back of this machine, slamming the door shut. The tail of the helicopter rose up. It did not *lift* up, but it did move forward toward the Icefall, where it plunged out of sight, as did my heart, because I knew he was not coming back.

Madan:

When I flew over Camp One they tied a rag to an ice ax to show me which way the wind was blowing, and they marked a spot for me to land. I later heard they used Kool-Aid. I saw the one little spot on the snow. It was too slopey, so I just moved a little farther to the left, where I decided to land. I said, "Now, God, you make it possible for me."

We were between two *big* crevasses. There were only a few feet on either side of the helicopter. The crevasses were dark blue. You could fit a whole house in them. And I found out there were two sick people. I was not giving any attention to them. I couldn't move my hand from the control, and I didn't want to move my head. That could affect my judgment. I said, "Only one," and they finally understood.

I took off very nicely and dropped the guy at Base Camp. But he was not the Beck. So I went back for the Beck.

That mission was specially requested for the Beck. It was

really a very, very difficult mission. There was no room for the helicopter to move if something went wrong. There were high winds—tail winds. You want head winds that give you extra lift.

And I had to land as close as possible to them. To walk fifty meters they need an hour. I only had a few minutes of fuel.

We stood there maybe five minutes. We didn't say anything, because there was nothing to say. And then I heard one of the most beautiful sounds I have ever heard in my entire life, that *whap! whap! whap!*—the distinctive chop of a helicopter. Long before we could see this thing we could hear it claw its way up that two-thousand-foot wall, once again this same lone man rising into view. He moved up the valley with greater authority.

With the same consummate skill he lay those skids down again. Not waiting, I hot-footed across there and dove into the back of this machine. They slammed the door and one more time the helicopter tail went up and we moved toward the precipice, crevasses gliding by beneath the skids.

We crested the edge and then went screaming down that face with the blades whipping around above us, trying to grab hold of cold, heavy, dense air that would provide lift. The machine felt alive beneath us as it pulled us out of the dive, and we knew we were safe.

We retrieved Makalu at Base Camp and put him back in. We got the copilot and put him back in. We got all the gear that Madan had stripped off this machine, and we put it back in.

That's when I discovered that when Madan returned to get me, he was flying the Squirrel on just seven minutes of fuel.

Madan is to me the most extraordinary person in this story, because he didn't know me at all. He didn't know my family, and he has his own family, for whom he is the sole provider. We were separated by language, by culture, by religion, by the entire breadth of this world, but bound together by a bond of common humanity.

This man will never have to wonder again whether he has a brave heart.

Madan:

I had a talk with the Beck on the way back to Katmandu. He was very excited, crying and patting me on the back. He was crying and saying, "You saved my life."

Peach later would write Madan, thanking him again for his extraordinary act of courage in plucking me off the mountain. I later learned from Madan that in all the hundreds of times he had rescued individuals in the Himalayas, this was the first time he'd been so thanked.

Maybe we all just take our heroes for granted.

Eight

David Breashears and others told me as we came down the mountain that all those deaths on Everest, and my own unlikely revival, were a major international news story. "Seaborne" Weathers's battered profile would appear on page one of *The New York Times*'s May 14 editions.

But the tragedy's resonance outside the climbing community and our families did not hit me until we landed at Tribhuvan. Reporters, most of them Japanese, began banging on the sides of the helicopter the moment we stopped. Flashbulbs were popping like crazy.

I really wasn't ready to meet the press. I felt and smelled and looked like the inside of an overripe Dumpster, and I had hardly come to terms myself with what had just occurred. Moreover, I was dressed in full mountain gear, boots and coat and all, not the most comfortable getup for a morning press conference in steamy Katmandu.

To my relief, the first person there as the helicopter door opened was David Schensted from the embassy. He introduced himself and then hustled me past the microphones and cameras and off to the Ciwek Clinic in Katmandu, where an American physician, Dr. David Schlim, would examine me.

While I was at Schlim's clinic, I also took advantage of my first chance to call home to Peach. Until that moment, she hadn't been given a clear description of exactly what had happened. I explained that although I was pretty well bunged up, I thought that I was going to be okay. She told me that my younger brother, Dan, who is a physician and at the time was in charge of the emergency room at Medical City Hospital in Dallas where I also practice, was on his way to Nepal. This was especially welcome news: I had begun to wonder how I was going to get home with no hands.

Peach:

I deeply love my husband and always have. But when Beck left for Mount Everest in March of 1996—he spent our twentieth anniversary there—I decided this was the last time he would run away from us. Beck was living only for his obsessions, and I saw no further hope of making our marriage work. I simply would not live my life that way any longer.

Beck seemed selfishly determined to either kill himself or get himself killed. He'd never admit this, but I think he went to Everest half convinced that he was going to die there. I sensed he was scared, even at the airport. I don't know that I'd ever seen him really scared before. He didn't articulate it, but you can just look at someone and tell. The body language, everything.

When Beck went away on these trips we *never* heard from him. Weeks would pass with no word. We all could have been wiped out in a tornado and Beck would not have known.

But this time he kept the lines open. I remember he called home on May 4 to tell us that after a month on the mountain they all finally were ready to climb it. Both Meg and I spoke to him.

I got faxes from him at least every other night. He wasn't so self-assured. Wasn't having as good a time. Moaning and groaning a little bit. Mr. Bulletproof was scared, and he needed to communicate. I thought, If you didn't want to talk to me here, why do you want to talk to me when you're there? Something about this simply doesn't make sense to me.

When he didn't hear back from me, he was concerned. "Why didn't I hear from you?" Actually, I would type up faxes for him, but you couldn't always get them through.

Of course, the real question was: Why did he have to do this in the first place?

While Beck was away, I watched a PBS program about this Scotswoman who had died climbing in the mountains. Her husband later took their two children back to the Himalayas so they could see where their mother died.

I remember thinking at the time, Fat lot of good that's going to do them, telling a four-year-old and a two-year-old, "Mommy's up there in the clouds."

I thought, That'll sure make them feel better. "Mommy was such a brave person." That's not going to help them when they fall down and skin their knees.

On Friday night, May 10, I received a brief call from Madeleine David in New Zealand. She said that Beck had not made it to the summit with the rest of the climbers, but that he was fine, and that they all were now coming down the mountain. There was nothing in her voice to alarm me. Yet after the conversation, I couldn't sleep. I moved from my bedroom into the den, and slept on the couch the rest of the night.

When she called again the next morning to report Beck was dead, all I felt was shock. My worst nightmare had come true. But I couldn't respond. It was the same as when you break your leg. Numb. I couldn't cry. I just kept thinking, Oh my God, what will I do now? My children suddenly had no father, so there was a fair amount of anger there, too.

I was alone in the house with our son, Beck, a junior in high school, who was asleep in his room. Our daughter, Meg, who was in the eighth grade, had spent the night at her school, chaperoning a group of younger children on a sleep-over.

I didn't want to have to tell either of my children that their father was dead, and so I tried to postpone doing so. Instead of going into Beck's room and awakening him with the news, I first made several telephone calls.

Instinct rules when a catastrophe strikes. My instinct that morning was to draw in my strength. So I called my brother Howie in Atlanta, and our Dallas friends: Terry and Pat White, Garrett and Cecilia Boone, Jim and Marianne Ketchersid, Linda Gravelle and Victoria Bryhan. I also called Beck's younger brother, Dan. Most of them came over at once. Through the morning, I reached out to several more dear friends. I needed these people around me.

They were my friends and Beck's friends, people to whom I repeatedly had turned for help and strength over the past ten years. They were loyal to both of us.

Once they arrived and I had no further excuse for delaying, I went to my son, woke him up, and told him that his father had been killed. Bub said something like "You've got to be kidding." He didn't cry. Bub never cries when you expect him to. He always cries later, at the funeral.

Bub:

I know a lot of people were afraid my Dad would get hurt on Everest. But I really hadn't paid that much attention. There was nothing new about Dad being gone to climb mountains. I may have had a twinge of foreboding—Everest has a weight that no other mountain has—but to be honest, I think I was somewhat blissfully ignorant.

Then I woke up that morning with these words: "Your father has been killed." My mom told me and turned away and left the room.

I thought, "All right, weird dream." Then I realized what she had said. I didn't know what to feel. More an absence of feeling than feeling. I got up. My mom's friends were all bawling. I walked around the rest of the morning wide-eyed, my jaw open. I wasn't in denial, I was just numb.

I remember there was a lot of talk about how to tell my sister what had happened. Everyone agreed that neither my mom nor I should drive, so Mom's friend Linda Gravelle drove us over to Meg's school.

Meg:

My science teacher got me up an hour early. "Your mom's here," she said.

So I got ready and went downstairs. Everyone was looking at

me weird. I was like "Okay . . ." We walked outside, where Mom says, "Daddy died."

There was a moment of shock, like maybe this was a dream. Then I burst into tears, dropped everything I was holding. I sank down. My brother picked up my stuff, and my mother got me into the car.

We drove back to the house, and I just sat in a chair in the den, like in a dream. It wasn't really me, but someone watching me. Eventually my friend Katherine Boone came over, and my other real, real good friends filtered over and we all sat in my room. I started saying, "I told him not to go! I told him to stay home! I begged him not to go to Everest."

A little while later, I was talking to another of my friends, Mariana Pickering, when I heard my mom on the phone saying, "Are you sure? Are you sure?" Then she turned around and said, "Beck's alive."

I burst into tears again. Such is my wont. I had this over-whelming feeling then that he'd be fine. I know my Dad. If he lives through the initial thing—whatever it is—then he's going to hang on, because we're both really stubborn. If he'd held on to life all night on that mountain, he wasn't going to let go now.

The Saturday I died on Mount Everest was also to have been the day of Meg's first real date. The things some fathers will do to keep their daughters away from boys. I had a lot of class, and all of it was low.

Nine

Peach:

I now know that Madeleine David probably was trying to prepare me for the inevitable. Apparently everybody at the time thought Beck was dead, one way or the other. But all I registered was hope. There was a moment of relief and joy, then we all went straight into "How do we get him to safety?"

Emotions were luxuries for which I didn't have time. My focus was on just gluing it together, just keeping it going. I surely did want to become hysterical. I wanted to go to my room with the vapors. But if I'd done that then, my kids would have become hysterical, too. That was not a choice.

Cecilia Boone:

The house was *full* of people all day. Coming and going. Kids. Older people. I'll bet that at any given time there were twenty-five or thirty people there. Peach was right in the middle of it, even washing tie-dyed shirts!

Meg had brought them home from school that morning, as part of her project, and they needed to be washed in cold water or something. So while everyone's on the telephone, calling all over the place for help and advice what to do, Peach had these T-shirts in the washing machine!

Peach:

We were not worried about getting Beck off the mountain. We didn't know that was any kind of big deal, or what it entailed. We just knew he was in critical condition, and he probably was going to need better medical attention than what was available in Nepal. That was it.

So starting on Saturday and then on into Sunday—Mother's Day—everyone worked the telephones. Terry White, who is a hematologist and oncologist, and Jon Esber, a partner in Beck's pathology practice, organized a search for the nearest medical center staffed with U.S.-trained physicians. It turned out to be in Singapore.

Since we assumed Beck was frostbitten, Terry also led the search for a frostbite expert. The best one in the world was in Alaska, which we expected would be Beck's second stop after Singapore, once we got him out of Nepal.

Our search for a way to evacuate Beck began with Kay Bailey Hutchison, the junior Republican senator from Texas, whom several of us knew. Her office stayed in constant touch with us.

Linda Gravelle called our governor, George W. Bush. His

twin daughters had gone to school with Meg, as well as Linda's daughter, Gwyneth.

Linda Gravelle:

I called him on his private line in Austin and got his daughter, Jenna. I said, "I need to talk to your dad." She said, "Well, he's jogging," or something like that. I told her what had happened, and that it was very important he call me back.

He did, and told me that this was a federal matter, that he could not deal with it on the state level. I said, "I cannot believe you! This is someone you know and you won't even help me!"

He said, "I just can't do anything. I don't know what to tell you."

I was pretty mad. We've seen him since, and the subject does not come up.

Then somebody said, "We need to get a Democrat involved in this."

Peach:

Cappy and Janie McGarr are friends of ours who are close to Tom Daschle, the minority leader in the Senate. They contacted him at home that morning. Daschle contacted the State Department, which contacted the embassy in Katmandu, which assigned David Schensted to the matter, which resulted in Madan K.C. risking his life to save Beck's.

Madeleine David called me from New Zealand at about 10:00 P.M. Dallas time on Sunday night to report that Beck had been successfully airlifted off the mountain. He'd be in Katmandu within the hour. I was ticketed to fly out to Nepal the following night at eight-twenty. But now that Beck had been rescued and his brother Dan was due in Katmandu at any minute, Madeleine counseled me to cancel my flight. Beck and Dan probably would be headed home together before I could even get there.

About three hours later—around 1:30 A.M. on Monday— Beck himself called from Katmandu. It was a familiar time of night to hear from him. While we were courting and Beck was still in medical school, he often called me in the middle of the night. I was used to it.

What made this call different from any before or after was Beck's clear need to connect with me, to actually *talk* to me. It was unspoken, but I immediately sensed something completely different about my husband. He'd been transformed by something—I didn't yet know what—that went beyond a lucky brush with death. He'd had those before.

He assured me he was okay, and said he was being cared for by Dr. Schlim. I didn't know anything about the rescue, or how dangerous it was, until Beck explained some of it during this call. I also did not learn of his epiphany until the next day, when we were being interviewed for the *Today* show.

That's when Beck told the world about seeing the children and me in his mind. I was really surprised by it, and saddened, too, because it had required such a tragedy for that to occur. He had to nearly die before he opened his eyes.

After Schlim redressed my hands and gave me some antibiotics, I walked the block or so from his office to one of Katmandu's better hotels, the Yak & Yeti, and checked myself in.

If you think that you have stayed in a full-service hotel, I suggest you probably don't have a clue what full service can entail. The Yak & Yeti, aware of my helpless condition, was thoughtful enough to station a young man in the hall outside my room, in case I needed to have my fanny wiped. Fortunately, I did not have to involve him. I hadn't eaten in days, which helped considerably.

A short time later, as I rested in my room, reflecting on my recent experience with the random quality of living and dying, my brother, Dan, appeared at the door, carrying a suitcase that contained a full complement of emergency room paraphernalia, as well as every drug known to man. I don't know if he had enough equipment to cut my heart out and put it back in, but he wasn't lacking much.

Dan also brought me a couple of changes of clothing

I was elated to see him, and he was pretty worked up, too. We hadn't exchanged but a few words before he blurted out, "Don't you ever, *ever* again do anything that gets you on television!"

Dan:

Over the years, I've had the responsibility many, many hundreds of times to share devastating news with others. But I had never received any before. It's a lot different on the receiving end.

The phone rang at 7:22 A.M. that Saturday morning. I was asleep, and before I could pick up the receiver the call rolled over to voice mail. I immediately went into the next room and called Peach, who abruptly said, "Beck's dead." She said she'd talk to me later.

I began screaming, which awakened my wife, Brenda. Then she and I and her son, Robert, sat on the floor and prayed and cried for a couple of hours. I went and wrote a letter to Beck. It read, in part, "Words cannot describe how much I'll miss you. Throughout my life, whenever I tripped or fell you were there to pick me up . . . over and over again. Of all the people in my life, you impacted me most. Your love and support have always made the worst of times okay."

I later gave it to him.

Then we got the second phone call from Peach. All she could tell me was that he was in critical condition. I immediately decided to go there.

This part is hard to describe. Beck is sixteen months older than I. Growing up, he and I shared the same bedroom for fifteen or sixteen years. We also shared apartments in college and medical school. We probably are as close as any two brothers, although we don't really talk that much. I dearly love him.

I felt compelled to go to him. I didn't care where he was. I didn't really know where I was going, or how I would get there. But I figured I was going to find him.

I didn't trust that he would have adequate medical care in Nepal, so I took a suitcase to the emergency department and explained to my head nurse what had transpired. I told her that I wanted as much medical equipment as possible packed in that suitcase. So the nursing staff gathered IVs, splints, bandages, catheters, medication. I went to the pharmacy and got morphine and Demerol.

Lufthansa was the only airline that flew from Dallas to Nepal, and the agent did not want to book me one way to Katmandu on no notice. That is not an innocent-sounding trip. I had to explain the situation to the agent's supervisor, that I was going to Nepal to find my brother. They booked me on a flight that left Dallas about seven that Saturday night.

I flew to Frankfurt, Germany, where I had a six-hour layover before connecting to Dubai and then on into Katmandu. In all, it took me thirty-some hours to get there, so I arrived in Katmandu around noon on Monday. I think that was just about an hour after Beck had arrived by helicopter from Mount Everest.

I did not have a clue where he was. The first thing I did was explain to the customs people exactly what I had with me, why I was there and what I intended to do. They were very polite and as helpful as they could be. They gave me a one-week visa, and I headed for a hotel.

I had just checked in when to my surprise a hotel employee told me some people were trying to find me. They were two employees from Adventure Consultants, who took me to David Schlim's office. This all happened very quickly. Within an hour of my arrival in Katmandu, I was talking to David Schlim.

I really liked him. He told me that he had examined the Taiwanese climber, Makalu Gau, who looked a lot worse than Beck. Schlim said he thought that at least one of Beck's hands was going to be okay. He also said Beck was not ill, systemically, that he had only third- and fourth-degree cold injuries to his extremities.

David and I talked for maybe half an hour, and then he personally took me over to the Yak & Yeti, which was just around the corner from his clinic. I had assumed Beck was in a hospital, and it wasn't until David walked me past a young man standing at Beck's door and into his room that it dawned on me that this was not a hospital at all, but a hotel.

Beck was still in his climbing clothes, except for his boots. He smelled like a burn patient. Having cared for many such victims over the years, I recognized the smell of dead tissue.

From the get-go Beck and I had markedly different perspectives.

He was very, very happy to be alive, to be back from the dead. Very upbeat. But I focused on his injuries, which were devastating.

I knew he'd require amputation. There was no doubt. His right hand was stone-cold dead. Already the skin was retracting around the bones. It looked like it had been stuck in an incinerator and left there.

I had brought a lot of pain medication with me, but Beck didn't need it. Once you recover from a third- or fourth-degree burn, or freeze, there isn't much pain. The nerves are all dead.

His left hand looked better. I really thought he'd only lose the ends of his fingers—a distal phalanx amputation.

Without the use of his hands, Beck was helpless, which meant we established a relationship we'd never had before. I took care of his every body function. I did that gladly. He was skinny as a rail.

That afternoon I received a visitor from the Japanese embassy. He asked if I would meet with Yasuko Namba's family. I of course said that I would, although it was not a meeting that I relished. The man from the embassy had brought a small box of chocolates as a gift to honor the occasion.

When Dan and I were returning from dinner that night, I saw a group of Japanese sitting at a table near the main entrance to the Yak & Yeti. I knew instantly that they were Yasuko's family: her husband, her brother and two friends.

They very much wanted to know about her and her last moments. I really didn't know what to tell them. I searched for anything that might comfort them. But for one of the very few times in my life, the easy stream of words simply wouldn't come. At some level I felt guilty standing there, alive, when Yasuko was gone. I couldn't even offer meaningful consolation.

Ten

My strongest impressions during the two days Dan and I spent in Katmandu were of contrasts. One minute I had been as good as dead on that cold, sterile mountain; the next, I was safe and warm in Katmandu, which teems with life.

I remember looking out the window of my ground-floor room into a beautiful garden. There were flowers and birds flying around, a jarring contrast to Everest. One night they held a huge formal party in the garden, very fancy with bright lights. It was a scene of rampant life enveloping me, even as my thoughts turned again and again to the five people I knew pretty well who were frozen dead on Everest.

I also noticed another type of contrast, now that I resembled some creature out of a B horror film. My hands were two huge balls of bandages. My face was red and swollen with black scabs of dead tissue, called eschars, covering my nose and cheeks.

The Japanese in Katmandu utterly ignored me. It was as if I

had not so much as a hair out of place. On the other hand, I recall walking into the hotel hallway where a Nepalese housekeeper was mopping the floor. She took one look at me and froze, her mouth agape, her mop clattering to the floor.

On our second day in Katmandu, after doing an interview with American television at one of the government buildings, I encountered a senior Nepalese official walking with his Gurka guard. I fascinated (or was it repelled?) him. He walked up to within three inches of my face and stared me up and down as if I were some sort of anthropology exhibit. He wasn't the least bit shy about his curiosity.

Dr. Schlim took one more look at me before we left. While I was at his clinic I was debriefed by Elizabeth Hawley, who'd rumbled up in her old Volkswagen. Hawley is something of a legend as the unofficial historian of mountain climbing in Nepal. Anyone who comes back from the mountains with a story must submit to a detailed grilling.

The Lufthansa flight home—we splurged on first-class seats—was long and, for the most part, uneventful. Dan and I set some sort of high-altitude record for repeatedly stuffing two adults into tiny airliner bathrooms. In Frankfurt, where we had a layover, I was surprised to be approached by a young woman from TV journalist Diane Sawyer's staff. She asked if I'd agree to a live satellite interview with Sawyer—immediately. I agreed automatically, almost without thinking. It wouldn't have occurred to me to say no.

Then on to Dallas. As we taxied to the gate, finally home, a fellow passenger who'd been drinking heavily for hours started yelling, "I'm never going to leave fucking home again! I'm *never* going to leave!" He was pretty emphatic.

I toyed with asking why he'd stolen my lines.

As we walked off the plane we were immediately turned through a door adjacent to the gangway. My escort said it would be easier to handle the crowd of reporters if I were willing to ride a wheelchair through the lounge. I agreed to do it.

We met briefly with the press; Bub read a statement my family had prepared. I was just incredibly grateful to be back. I told them it wasn't Kansas, but it was home.

Peach waited for me in the VIP lounge. Someone from Lufthansa had given me a rose, which I placed in her hand. I saw love in her eyes, but also a look that said, I'm not sure where we're going to be when we get back to the house. At that instant, all I wanted to do was hold her. I wasn't thinking of anything else. I wanted to smell her hair and feel her face against mine. I had a sense that I was finally back, no longer just journeying.

Peach:

I just felt tremendous relief he was home. I was totally unbothered by his appearance. He didn't look good, but Beck is Beck. I was just taking things in order, one crisis at a time. He's sick, so let's deal with that. I must have liked him at some time.

Beck would say that he always loved me. But my definition of love did not include what I felt he'd done to me and especially to our children. If he loved me, I thought, he would never, never, ever have done this.

I had long ago convinced myself that my relationship with my family might be salvageable if I refocused. If I could get the mountain-climbing part behind me, I believed that we could work it out. Now that the mountain years definitely were over, it was time to test that hypothesis.

On the flight home, the joy at having survived mellowed into a sense of relief I was off the mountain and coming back. But there was apprehension. What about my wounds, the future, Peach? At that point, all were unknowns.

I don't have a lot of self-confidence, and most of the time I don't feel that wonderful. Chasing up and down mountains had helped keep that problem at bay.

Now the future had suddenly become very uncertain, and I'm not wild about uncertainty. I worried about being crippled, *how* crippled; how things were going to stay together at work. I realized, too, that Peach had said I was going to get myself killed, or maimed, and here I was!

I was not looking forward to that conversation.

That first evening at home Peach told me the years of climbing and obsession had driven her and the children away from me. She'd had all she could stand, and had decided while I was on the mountain that as soon as I got back into Dallas, she was going to inform me our marriage was over, and that she would then leave.

"Damn you for doing this to me," she added.

I told her I knew that I was to blame for everything that had happened to me, and that I'd have to bear the consequences. She did not have to stay through this—certainly not out of pity. I'd never blame her for leaving. I'd understand and never, ever speak ill of that decision.

She said, "No, I'm going to give you one year. If you're a truly different person at the end of that year, we'll talk about it."

I decided at that moment that I'd dedicate all my obsession, drive and determination, and by the end of that year I truly would be a different person. Somehow, I'd reclaim not only her love, but the trust I'd lost. Even at that moment I believed Peach still loved me, but the pain in her eyes eloquently expressed her lack of trust in me.

One singular joy of that first day back was a sip of a really fine single-malt scotch, a gift from our friend Dan Lewis. The next day I ate a small bowl of Blue Bell homemade vanilla (not the French) ice cream. It was absolutely wonderful. In the first week home, I went to see the alien invasion movie *Independence Day* with Bub and Meg. As we sat in the darkened theater, they watched the movie as I, sitting between them, stared at my two children and was supremely happy.

Peach was under incredible stress. Anybody we'd ever met in history decided now was the moment to call up and quiz her on something, or try to get involved. They didn't realize our need for some peace to get control of our existence.

I felt like someone had taken me out and beaten me up. I'd lost the thirty pounds I'd purposefully gained in preparation for climbing Everest. My body was *tired*. I also developed a ripping infection from the IV that had been placed in my right arm on the mountain, an added memento of the climb. It had started to swell and was painful. We didn't know exactly what the germ was, other than it didn't respond to a number of antibiotics until we finally found one that worked.

Despite my brother Dan's opinion, I at first was hopeful I'd only lose the tips of my right fingers, and that the damage to my left hand might be trivial. Perhaps I'd need an amputation down to the first joints or possibly to the palm. But I'd end up with a working left hand, more or less, and at least *something* on the right.

That was before my hand surgeon, Mike Doyle, ordered a scan that showed both hands were dead; there was no circulation at all. Soon thereafter my right hand began to self-amputate. Greg Anigian, my plastic surgeon, was concerned that the tendons were going to snap. Surgery was necessary *now*.

I began slipping. I was full of medicine. I realized I probably was going to lose both my hands, and possibly wasn't going to work again. I didn't know if I were going to be able to continue providing my family an income. That was vitally important to me, because it meant I was contributing. Before Everest, that was one of the ways I rationalized that I was doing something good.

Peach:

After Beck learned he was going to lose both hands, he asked me, "Will this make a difference to you?"

I said, "Well, no." But the truth of the matter was that I wasn't sure.

I grew depressed; not the old black-dog darkness, but what I believe psychiatrists call a reactive depression; in other words, a very reasonable response to a world of problems.

I brooded about a future of being alone, sitting and watching daytime television by myself in a custodial venue. Not an attractive prospect. I remember being given catalogs for prosthetic devices, looking at stuff to help you turn pages with your teeth. I wondered if I'd ever eat another hamburger, or would I have to take gruel through a straw for the rest of my life? And since I'd become seriously depressed twice before, I was scared of the potential for that to happen again, too.

You could say that I saw a very limited upside to the situation.

It was about then that I realized I needed to do a couple of things. One was not to fall apart. I had to find something to live for each day, to think about. For the foreseeable future, I needed a sense of something concrete that I could do physically.

So, I made a whole series of decisions, mostly having to do with avoiding the pit. I was not going to feel sorry for myself under any circumstance, and I was not going to dodge responsibility for what I'd done and the harm I'd inflicted. I felt pretty guilty. If possible, I was going to redeem myself in Peach's eyes. Whatever it took, I was going to give it a shot.

I could not then have imagined the avenue to redemption that ultimately opened to me, or the trials that lay ahead for both of us. Suffice it to say that when the shadow of a second life-and-death crisis suddenly fell over the Weathers household that summer, it was my time to give back so much that I'd stolen away.

Dan, Beck and
Kit Weathers,
1951.

Howard, Margaret (Peach)
and Wayne Olson, 1951.

Beck and Peach with Beck II,
1979.

PART TWO

Eleven

It is a slander that we Southerners waste all the good names on our dogs.

My father, Arthur Kitchings Weathers, was determined that each of his sons would have a given name with some heft to it. So his firstborn became Arthur Kitchings Weathers, Jr.; I was named Seaborn Beck Weathers; and my younger brother is James Daniel Weathers. It is not my father's fault that we are known as Kit, Beck and Dan.

I was born on December 16, 1946, in Griffin, Georgia, about thirty miles south of Atlanta. My mother, the former Emily Williams Beck, also was born in Griffin, a textile-manufacturing center of approximately 25,000 inhabitants. Griffin, which has been home to mother's family for six generations, long ago was famous as a flower-growing center—the town once referred to itself as the Iris Capital of the World. More recently, Griffin served as the setting for the film *Driving Miss Daisy,* which won the Oscar for best picture of 1989.

My father is a native of Cairo (Kay-Ro), Georgia, a small town in the southwestern part of the state, where his father, Jesse Seaborn Weathers, served as school superintendent and postmaster, and practiced law as well. Dad majored in political science and law at Emory University in Atlanta. After his graduation in 1940, he came to Griffin as an official with the National Youth Administration, a New Deal agency set up to provide educational opportunity to young people. In his free time, he took flying lessons and earned a private pilot's license.

My mother graduated from the University of Georgia in 1940 with a biology degree, and returned home to Griffin to teach high school. She met her future husband, the would-be aviator, at a party. They were married on a Saturday night in May 1942.

Arthur and Emily spent their honeymoon on the road to Ocala, Florida, where my father would attend army air corps flight school. They paused occasionally along the way so he could teach her how to drive his Studebaker Champion.

He expected to see combat but instead was told he'd be a flight instructor, and spent the balance of the war years teaching other young men how to fly a variety of combat aircraft, particularly P-38 fighters. My father is a gentle soul, and it probably was just as well he wasn't required to shoot at anybody.

After the war, he sold life insurance in Albany, Georgia, for a while, and worked part-time at a car rental agency owned by my mother's uncle. Fate then intervened in the form of the 1948 Soviet blockade of West Berlin, which changed everything for my father, and thus for his family. Lieutenant Weathers was recalled to the newly organized U.S. Air Force, and was to have participated in the Berlin airlift until a last-minute change in orders sent him to Japan and the U.S. Army of Occupation there. Dad left for Japan in August of 1948, a week after my brother Dan was born.

That made Dad three-for-three. Because of his military obligations, he hadn't been home when Kit and I were born, either.

Many of my earliest recollections are of Japan, where my mother brought my brothers and me in the spring of 1949 aboard an old tub, the S.S. *Gen. M. M. Patrick,* an experience that to this day she scorns as among the worst in her life. The trip began with me getting lost in the Atlanta train station—I slipped my leash and was later recovered happily seated in the colored waiting area—and deteriorated from there.

On the voyage from Seattle, Dan developed a fever and had difficulty breathing. Both Kit and I were seasick. Mother decided the *Patrick*—she called it the *Mickey Mouse Patrick*—was too unsafe for us to leave our stateroom, so that is where she stayed with the three of us for the better part of nineteen days at sea. She refused even to participate in fire drills. When at last we disembarked (my parents happily reunited on the pier after an eight-month separation), little Dan in Mother's arms brought her adventure from hell to an appropriate close by eating her orchid corsage.

Our destination was Shiroi, a onetime golf resort the Japanese had converted into an airfield during World War II. The installation was located about twenty-five miles northeast of Tokyo. Because he had studied some law in college, my father was made base legal officer, among his other duties, and was known around Shiroi as "Judge."

Our first quarters at Shiroi was a Quonset hut infested with huge rats. They boldly came out each night to squeal and forage around the place. Even the big cat my parents borrowed in an effort to control the rodents was afraid of them. Arthur and Emily took turns watching out lest one of the furry devils bite us as we slept. My brother Kit thought the rats were pets.

Japanese exterminators visited us regularly, with no greater impact on the vermin population than the cowardly cat. I knew them as the "latmen," because of their trouble with *r*'s.

I liked the Japanese gardeners, especially one old guy who didn't have the vaguest hint about English. Of course, I spoke no Japanese, but that didn't stop us from becoming buddies. I'd squat down next to him while he worked, chattering away.

I found one gardener's lunch one day, fish heads and rice, and swallowed the works. My mother had me wormed.

One compensation for our down-market billet was abundant and cheap domestic help. Three Japanese women, Magai ("Margo"), Shizeko and Miyoko worked for us from eight in the morning until ten at night. The first two cleaned and cooked in return for their meals, and Shizeko received $8 a month— Margo was free, part of war reparations, believe it or not. Miyoko, whom Dad paid $12 a month, was a wizard at the sewing machine. All my mother had to do was point to a little boy's outfit she liked in a magazine, and Miyoko would whip up three exact copies to size for Kit and Dan and me, all in the same color (usually bright) to make it easier for my mother to keep track of us in crowds.

I have two other lasting recollections of Japan. One is of the four months Dan spent at Tokyo General Hospital in a steam tent, being treated for bronchial asthma. His recovery was complicated when a nurse knocked the steam kettle over his foot, causing a painful burn. The doctors nearly were forced to amputate.

The other is of air raid drills at Shiroi. It seemed like every other night we'd give the rats the run of the house while we went outside and hunkered down in the dark. I'm not sure who they expected to attack us—rogue elements of the Imperial Air Force, flying kites?

We sailed back to the United States in 1951 via the S.S. *Gen. E. D. Patrick,* a somewhat homier sister ship to the *Mickey Mouse.* This transport featured enclosed decks and a nursery, where Mother could park us boys from time to time. The single somber note to an otherwise pleasant, ten-day voyage was the Korean War casualties we carried home with us, stacked in caskets aboard the *Patrick.*

My father's next assignment was Dobbins Air Force Base in Atlanta. We rented an apartment across the street from an elementary school, where I entered the first grade as a five-year-old.

I probably should have gone into kindergarten, but I wouldn't have any part of that. I wanted to go to real school. My eyes were underdeveloped, however, and the weak muscles made it difficult for me to track the page during reading. As a result, I was placed among the remedial readers, which actually thrilled me; I loved to read and this gave me more opportunity to try it.

The return to Georgia afforded me my first real opportunity to get to know my grandparents. My father's father, for whom I was named, was extremely reserved. As my own dear old dad grows older, he has come to resemble his father more and more, both in appearance and demeanor.

Dad met his grandfather on only one occasion, when he was placed on a train to ride across Georgia to a meeting of Confederate Civil War veterans. My great-grandfather (I'm told) was resplendent in his Confederate uniform that day. I'm reminded that in the South Memorial Day was once celebrated as Confederate Veterans Day and the Civil War was known as the War of Northern Aggression.

The personality in that generation was my maternal grandmother, Ethel Beck, who was always upbeat and chatty. My grandmother also enjoyed some local renown for having begun one of the first Girl Scout troops in Georgia. Girl Scout founder Juliette Low even sent her a letter of appreciation.

The Weathers side of the family put great store in decorum. Coarseness we take for granted today did not exist in that household. The word *gosh,* for example, would have given my paternal grandmother, Nancy, a heart attack. Even I had the sense not to use *gosh* or *darn* in front of her. Of course, I also didn't know any words stronger than that.

My favorite was Ethel's husband, my grandfather Lewis Beck, whom we all knew as Pappy. He was educated as a textile engineer at Georgia Tech, and oversaw the operations of several mills in Griffin before retiring to raise flowers, a decision forced in part by Pappy's weakness for strong waters. He was in any case a demon gardener—Jackson and Perkins, the rose people, often asked him to try out their new hybrids—and also maintained an enormous library with books on every subject imaginable. Pappy was a Renaissance man.

One of my greatest joys was for him to read Joel Chandler Harris's Uncle Remus stories to me. He did all the characters, Br'er Rabbit, Br'er Fox and the rest, in perfect dialect, as Chandler wrote them, no mean feat. I'd later give baby-sitters the same books to read to me. They'd quickly become tongue-tied, so I'd read the stories to them.

Pappy was a staunch Methodist. I recall one Christmas he and I took a walk that brought us past the First Baptist Church of Griffin, where Peach and I later would be married. Glancing up at the imposing and quite beautiful structure, I asked my grandfather if this was where God lived.

"No," Pappy replied, "but the Baptists think he does."

In 1954, the Weathers family packed up again, this time for Brooks Air Force Base near San Antonio. My mother was horrified at the idea of moving to what she presumed was the nether edge of the civilized world. I, who was then in the second semester of my second-grade year, was delighted by the expectation of finally owning my own pony, which I'd ride to school each day and hitch to a rail, the way I'd seen in the movies.

We both were mistaken, yet San Antonio turned out to suit us fine. I didn't get a pony, but there were millions of horned toads around, and I don't think I've ever enjoyed anything more than chasing after them. There was also a huge field of sunflowers behind our house. Daily, I would take a stick out there to do combat with the sunflower people. Hopelessly outnumbered though I was, I could have soldiered on indefinitely. The sunflowers probably would have persevered eternally, too, had they not eventually been plowed under.

I sailed effortlessly through the San Antonio schools during our five-year stay there, less a testament to my brilliance than to the quality of public education in Texas. In my seventh-grade class there were at least a couple of guys who went home to the wife and kids each night.

Dan:

I've always admired Beck. He just seemed to carve his own path. I sensed that even as a small child, and was grateful for a big brother to follow and to emulate, which I did. And I've liked him most of the time. He's real headstrong and not always easy to get along with. My mom always says we fought like cats and dogs when we were young.

I remember the competition was fierce. Beck was determined to always win—and he did. It didn't matter what it was. He was better.

Beck's gears are always grinding. He has a need to be in the limelight. He's always talking and intellectualizing and telling stories. There's a lot of bravado there. I like the Beck who's quieter, who asks me, "How are you feeling?"

Next stop on the military-brat circuit was Dhahran, Saudi Arabia, which the reader likely will recall is the U.S. Air Force base where nineteen American airmen were killed in a June 1996 terrorist truck-bomb attack.

Back in the 1950s, Dhahran was an isolated airstrip, a few low buildings and a collection of about forty concrete-block duplexes set about with oleander trees. Nearby was an ARAMCO oil installation.

My father was transferred to Dhahran in November of 1958. Mother followed with us boys on Easter weekend, 1959. We flew out of Charleston, South Carolina, on Good Friday on a Lockheed Constellation, making stops in Bermuda, the Azores and Tripoli before landing in Saudi Arabia on Easter Sunday. The plane was filled with Iranian pilots on their way home from training in the States. My mother was the only female aboard.

We discovered Saudi Arabia was hot and flat and nearly featureless under an unremitting sun, sort of like North Texas in the summer. My grandmother Beck sent us an audiotape of rain falling just to remind us of the sound. But Dhahran also was a great place to be a kid. There were free movies every night at the officers' club, and the community swimming pool was directly across from our house. There weren't many schoolmates my age in the three-room Quonset-hut school I attended (thirteen kids total in grades seven and eight), but enough for plenty of volleyball and softball games. There was Little League, too, with five or six teams made up mostly of the ARAMCO oil workers' sons. I was catcher for the air force contingent, the Dhahran Flyers, and was league home-run king one year.

The Persian Gulf was just a few miles away. We'd go fishing in the gulf, where I also learned to water-ski. I can't imagine a more magical setting for night water-skiing than the Persian Gulf. Phosphorescent plankton glow bright under the moonlight in the prop wash and in your skis' wake, causing a huge light show to funnel up as you crisscross behind the boat. Even swimming stirs up the little buggers.

I joined the Boy Scouts, too. Practicing our forest skills, of course, was difficult. Mostly, we'd go and squat in the desert. Out of that experience also grew one of my life's lingering annoyances. Every Sunday for a year I worked to earn a God and Country Award, a sort of super merit badge in the form of a little shield—white with a blue cross on it, as I remember. I worked for it, and I wanted it, but they never sent it to me. That probably explains my later drift into secular humanism.

Dharhan, like Shiroi, offered my mother the welcome amenity of cheap domestic help, a Somali houseboy named Mohammed, whom we shared with the Skinner family on the other side of our duplex. Otherwise, the Arabian desert was no garden of delight for adults, especially if you took your religion seriously, or enjoyed a restorative zizz at sundown. King Saud was reasonably tolerant of us infidels, but he would not brook any external Christian symbols or insignia (church services were held in the unmarked community center, behind closed doors), nor was a drop of booze permitted on the base, a real hardship for some of my teachers.

It was not uncommon for the air force to send personnel to Dharhan for precisely that reason, to confront and defeat their inner devils.

Over at ARAMCO, however, amateur stills flourished; I think every family had one installed under their house. The joke was that if your plumbing stopped up, forget about it. You could wait a month for a maintenance guy to show. But if you called to report problems with your still, help arrived at once. This was only prudent; a maladjusted or balky still could, and occasionally did, erupt explosively.

The Dhahran base school ran only to the eighth grade. My brother Kit, who was a sophomore when we arrived, tried a year of correspondence school with some other kids, but that didn't work out. So he, and then I, shipped out of Saudi Arabia to attend high school. Kit went first to a boarding school in Wiesbaden, then to an air force dependents' school in Dreux, France, southwest of Paris, where I followed him two years later.

The school at Dreux was excellent, with very high academic standards. But besides a little wine-drinking adventure I got into there with some of my buddies, the most memorable moments of my one year at Dreux took place on vacations.

At Christmas break, we all flew to Ethiopia to go on safari. Protected from the numerous local bandits by heavily armed escorts, we hunted gazelle, guinea hens and wild boar, as I recall. I shot a gazelle, which was a thrill, even though I felt a little guilty about it, looking into his big brown eyes.

We also visited the Holy Land as a family. The most vivid recollection I have of that trip is an incident at the Church of the Nativity in Bethlehem. As I was photographing the star on the church's floor, I stepped back into a rack of candles and lit myself afire. "Holy smokes!" yelled brother Kit, indulging a weakness for puns and word play we all get from our father. Even I, the semiscorched object of Kit's humor, had to laugh.

After approximately two and a half years in Dhahran, now Lieutenant Colonel Weathers was transferred again, this time to Sheppard Air Force Base near dusty Wichita Falls, Texas, my father's final posting before retirement in 1964. Kit by this time had decided his life's work would be rock and roll. My mother naturally differed, and coerced him into accepting her idea of destiny—dentistry.

It was a "you can be a rock star after you finish dental

school" sort of thing. So my older brother enrolled at Midwestern State University in Wichita Falls, and then transferred to Dad's alma mater, Emory, to learn to drill, yank and polish, according to mother's wishes.

Kit:

We were a fairly normal family—for the military. Our parents didn't put up with any BS. We had to stand up straight and observe all the standard military stuff. At home we toed the line, observed all the rules. We didn't dare not do what was supposed to be done.

Our parents always encouraged us, though, told us we could be anything we wanted to be, anything we set our minds to. My family has always been very goal oriented. I remember we were given IQ tests. My mother took me aside and told me I had a special responsibility to succeed because I had the highest IQ. I've never discussed this with Beck or Dan, but I wouldn't be surprised if she said the same thing to each of them.

Dan and Beck and I are all risk takers, which I think we got from that encouragement, and from my father. We all tend to drive too fast, for example. My youngest brother, Dan, got his airplane pilot's license. Beck climbed mountains. For twenty-five years, I had a hot-air balloon with fifteen-foot-tall teeth painted on its sides. Just got a new one. I also recently took up paracycling, which is a sort of motorized parachuting.

One of my other hobbies is rock and roll. I still play regularly in a group we call the Party Time Band.

Mother was the disciplinarian in our family. She, more than our father, tended to shape our lives. For instance, she knew she wanted us all in professions where we'd do well financially. When I showed an interest in building model airplanes, she said, "Well, you're so good with your hands, you should be a dentist." I was pretty young at the time. I think all along she had our lives mapped out for us.

The family unit was always important to her. Mother was very close to her brother and sister, and tried to maintain that closeness in our family as well. Family holidays matter a lot, as does keeping in touch. On the Mother's Day prior to Beck's incident on Everest, she sent each of her sons a Mother's Day gift, telling us, "Thanks for being such great sons."

Like all kids in military families, we couldn't afford to make close friends while we were growing up, because we moved around so much. I, for example, attended high school in four different countries. Also, my brothers and I weren't real close, but that was probably because I was the oldest by more than three years.

Of the three of us, I think I'm the most outgoing. I think of myself as very self-assured. Beck is much more introspective. He always seemed to have something on his mind. He looked more inside himself, not because he was afraid to have contact with people, I think; it just didn't seem to matter that much to him. Of the three of us, he was the deepest thinker.

I entered Burkburnett High School near Wichita Falls as a sophomore in the autumn of 1961. Education was an afterthought at Burkburnett—the kind of place where they held an annual junior-senior fight. They actually had organized fist-fights, which held little appeal for a five-eight, 127-pound bruiser such as myself. I stayed home on junior-senior fight day.

Despite my size, however, I didn't get picked on too much as a kid. I was clever enough to realize when Tharg should be left alone. Besides, I am a bleeder. I didn't see any merit in getting the bejabbers beat out of me by going toe to toe with someone seventy-five pounds heavier than I.

The classroom was quite a switch from Dreux. I remember one history teacher who couldn't correctly pronounce place names. Lacking any challenge there, I spent the ensuing three years making straight A's, more or less, as I honed the art of playing hooky. It became a point of pride with me that I did not put in one full five-day school week my entire senior year.

My size pretty much prevented me from continuing in sports at Burkburnett, as did my flat feet and poor vision. I had discovered on a camping trip in Europe that when you see a tree, you should also be able to see its leaves, not just a green blur. Since I had seen well enough to play baseball and other sports in Dhahran, I can only assume that the onset of my extreme near-sightedness (I'm also night blind) was age related.

For a while I would pull back the sides of my eyes to fore-shorten them, and thus improve my vision. I also borrowed my mother's glasses, until I finally admitted I needed my own at about age thirteen. I hated wearing them, but I never could tol-erate contact lenses of any sort. All I ever got were infections, exacerbated by multiple allergies.

But I did discover at Burkburnett the joys of acting, poetry interpretation and debate. I won a districtwide best-actor competition for my role in the school's production of *The Glass Menagerie*, and third place in a statewide poetry-reading contest.

Debate was another matter. I remember getting thoroughly waxed by the debate team from St. Mark's School in Dallas, which my son, Beck, would later attend. The subject had something to do with communism in Latin America. I can't remember if I was for or against it, but I do know that I put forth a less-than-compelling series of arguments.

My very first motorized vehicle was a Vespa GS motor scooter. It had tires slightly larger than the wheels on a roller skate. I'd flatten myself out on the seat, open the throttle and then hang on, catching June bugs in the face as the speedometer inched toward the Vespa's absolute upper limit, seventy miles per hour.

Then I graduated to use of the family Karmann Ghia. Kit already had slammed the little import into a bridge. Now it was my turn. My friends and I would drive like maniacs around the dirt farm roads near Sheppard. One time after a rain, I mistook a two-foot-deep wallow in the road for a wide puddle and plowed the Ghia right into it. When I opened the door, mud oozed over the sill into the car.

I was able to push the Ghia to the edge, but not out, of the hole. So I walked out to the nearby highway and hitched a ride from a trucker, who drove me down the road to a friend's house. He knew a farmer with a tractor who pulled the car out of the mud for me. Then a morning's worth of scrubbing and cleaning and voilà! The evidence was washed away, and my parents never found out. Until now.

For refreshments, we'd drive an hour north into Oklahoma and to a certain remote roadside establishment whose owner stayed in business, I believe, principally on the strength of his alcohol sales to minors. This was the sort of place where if you could say, "Scotch and wa-wa," they'd serve it to you.

We'd buy a couple cases of Jax, a barely potable regional brand, since defunct, which my buddies and I drank as we rumbled around, shooting rabbits. Any beer we didn't finish off we'd bury and then disinter for consumption on our next hunting trip, unbothered by the ugly things that can happen inside a bottle of beer when it sits in a shallow grave in 115-degree weather for a week or two.

Eventually, we tired of the two-hour-round-trip drive to Oklahoma to purchase just a six-pack or three of 3–2 beer—that is, beer with a 3.2 percent alcohol content, about the equivalent of old apple juice. So on one excursion I bought several cases and secreted them away in the family camper, which we rarely used. This, of course, was my father's signal to offer the camper for sale. When he took a potential buyer out one day to demonstrate its many features, Dad and his buyer found beer in drawers, closets and the fridge, everywhere I'd stuffed it.

Dad was angry with me. On the other hand, he didn't have to buy any beer for the next couple of months.

These halcyon days finally skidded to a close with my graduation from Burkburnett High in June of 1964. Hubristically, I sent applications to first-tier universities such as Duke and Rice, not understanding at the time how thoroughly undereducated I really was. They, of course, rejected me, probably to a chorus of hoots and guffaws as they did.

So I chose Midwestern State as Kit had, and began my college education in a summer-school English class. I recall the course was taught by a good professor. He stunned me with a *D* on my first graded assignment. My life passed before my eyes.

Twelve

I never have had a strong self-image, certainly not in my adult life. In high school, I considered myself pretty much a wimp. Bright dweeb says it pretty well.

Nor was I ever all that happy. I existed in what you might call a steady state; I could do my work and function day to day, but I was never at peace or happy or really ever felt good. Certainly from my college days forward, I always was off in the future somewhere, trying to get someplace so I could get out of whatever place I was. I was never able to be of the moment.

This was my mood, more or less, when my first depression descended in my freshman year at Midwestern. Anxiety and low self-esteem may have been my chronic companions, but the depression was acute. I didn't mention anything about it to anybody. I just crawled into bed and stayed there. If I admitted I was depressed, then I'd be admitting a weakness, which I wouldn't do. I also knew someone would want me to get help.

I'd have to talk to somebody about it, share the fact that I felt miserable. Then I'd be forced to deal with it, and I didn't want to do that.

But I did think about suicide. The pain and the feelings of hopelessness were that intense. After three or four months of this, I just sort of wandered out of it and began feeling a lot better—or at least not as bad. What didn't go away was a new certainty within me: Barring the unforeseen (a fatal accident or mortal disease), the black dog someday would return and overwhelm me, and I would die by my own hand.

Dan:

Beck and I have discussed his depression, and mine. I think Beck's emotional tone is not much different from mine. I see us very much as soulmates.

I struggle with lethargy, and therefore seek activities to energize me: working in the emergency room, exercising, flying airplanes. I do things to bump up my adrenaline.

I'm not sure which side of the family we get it from, but I think it's our mother's. Pappy drank, and I have a tendency toward alcoholism—medicating the bad feelings. I'm sure that's not too different from what my grandfather was doing.

He and Beck were a lot alike, too. There wasn't a subject Pappy couldn't talk about, and Beck's the same way. The only thing I've ever discussed with Beck that he was clueless about was emotions. He still doesn't get it, doesn't fully understand. This may be a survival issue with him, but he became so hyper-intellectual that it got him away from feelings. Beck has a huge wall, although it's a little lower now.

The depression did not interfere with my education. Once that summer-school English class taught me how ignorant I was, I settled down to work at Midwestern. Despite a six-week bout with mononucleosis my first semester—which also kept me in bed a good deal—I earned one *B*, in band, and the rest *A*'s. I dropped band after that, even though I enjoyed it, which tells you something about my nature. I wasn't going to take any subject unless I excelled in it.

I lived at home to save money, but I joined the Kappa Alphas to force myself into some sort of social life. I wasn't the reticent sort, but I knew that I wouldn't attend any college functions on my own. I certainly did not have the kind of personality to go barhopping in search of girls.

In return for the social boost, I upped the fraternity chapter's grade average a full point.

When one of my KA brothers remarked on the obvious and suggested I add some muscle through weight lifting, I took his suggestion and found that I really enjoyed the exertion. That seems to be a key word for me: *exertion.*

For the first time since Little League I had some sort of athletic achievement of which to be proud. Plus it bulked me up to about 165 pounds. It felt good to be one of the stronger guys in the fraternity.

Nevertheless, I remained preoccupied with tomorrow instead of today, which inevitably raised the issue of what I wanted that tomorrow to be. I prefer to be judged on what I can do, what skills I bring to the table, rather than who I am or may seem to be. Therefore I like subjects such as mathematics (no surprise), where at the end of an exercise there is an answer. Not so in English class. I hated the subjectivity of most liberal arts courses. With science, you know exactly where you're headed.

The law interested me for that reason; not courtroom oratory, but the noble sense that law codifies our humanity. It is structure. Some of the greatest intellectual struggles in history turned on issues of legal rights. That had enormous appeal to me. Still does.

I think I'd make a good contract lawyer, because I understand the nuances of how people try to lever each other. That's simply a grasp of tactics and strategy. I'd be a disaster at counseling people to understand their motivations. I know I'd project my concrete view of the world on them.

Medicine beckoned, too, and for a while I considered pursuing degrees in both disciplines. I'm most comfortable in a situation where the application of intelligence and hard work will yield a desired result in a fairly predictable way. Mountain climbing appealed to me, in part, for that reason. It also rewards the gradual accretion of skills and experience. You can lay out a plan to climb mountains the same way you can lay out a course of study in medical school.

Too bad one's personal life is not so easily managed.

In the end, I decided it would be a waste of time and effort to train as both a physician and a lawyer. I declared myself a premed student, principally because that preserved the most academic options for the longest time, and I pursued a double major in mathematics and chemistry, which required 160 semester hours of course credit to complete. A full scholarship for my final three years at Midwestern did wondrous things for my personal exchequer, but I still needed to work full-time one summer to cover my costs.

The job was long-haul trucking around Texas for Mayflower, the moving company (I was too young to drive interstate). The compensation was a pitiable $1.25 an hour, plus $4 a day for motels and a dollar for food. I'd hire high school kids and winos to pack a truckload for me in the afternoon, then drive all night—typically three or four hundred miles—to reach my destination by first thing the next morning. In this way, I logged about ninety hours a week, and shaved costs by sleeping in the truck and packing my own sandwiches.

Usually I'd push the big rigs until I was so tired I saw double, my clue that it was time to pull over and sleep. I recall that on one trip to Houston, I was asleep in the back of the truck on some furniture pads when I was awakened in the middle of the night by this tremendous noise. It was a locomotive, and it seemed to be coming straight for me. I couldn't remember where I was for a moment, then it dawned on me: Okay, I'm in the truck. *Where* did I put the truck? I knew I'd pulled off the road.

I thought to myself, You could not have parked this thing on a railroad track, could you?

By now the sound was right on top of me. The truck was starting to shake. I held my breath, and the train blew by, barely missing me, the truck and some poor guy's divans and end tables.

I need to be a little more careful, I thought, but did not connect the episode with any sort of death wish or my earlier depression.

It was not an enjoyable summer hauling furniture around in the Texas heat, but it certainly was instructive, an object lesson in the value of learning to use your mind instead of your back. By September I was more than happy to be hitting the books instead of the road, and for the next two summers I went to summer school.

Dan:

I followed Beck from Burkburnett to Midwestern. Our father retired and took a job with the FAA in Memphis. Mother, who had gotten her master's degree at Midwestern, was contracted to teach biology there for a year. I took her class, in fact. She and Beck and I lived together that year. The next year, Beck's last at Midwestern, he and I shared an apartment together. When he graduated, I transferred to the University of Texas at Austin, where I decided to study medicine, as well. Until that moment it had been a toss-up whether I would become a doctor, or a pilot like my father.

As I finished college, I, like many of my generation, developed a burning interest in further education. The Vietnam War focused many of us on the benefits of graduate school, if it entailed a military deferment.

My medical schools of choice were Duke, Tennessee and the University of Texas Southwestern Medical School in Dallas.

Southwestern both accepted me and offered me an academic scholarship. Next stop: Dallas.

That first summer before starting medical school I worked at the university as a computer programmer, assigned chores like transposing census tract data from one format to another. It was mind-bogglingly dull work, about as stimulating as schlepping furniture.

I found a suitable duplex apartment near campus and lived there alone my first year. My landlady was a sweet old soul, in her mid- to late-eighties, I guessed, still tough enough at that age to mow her own lawn, in the summer, with an old push mower. She occasionally cooked suppers for me, signal events in a life otherwise spent buried in the labors of first-year med school.

There was a huge amount of memorization, which I sort of plodded through, making grades from the ordinary to the very good. A student's success that first year hinges on whether he can develop an interest in what his professors are trying to hammer into him. The information itself often turns out to be a random series of facts with no discernible unifying themes.

In microbiology, for example, you might get a guy who talks for ten days on cholera, a disease I have yet to encounter in twenty-plus years of practice. I remember another professor wanted to spend a couple of days on osmosis across the toad bladder, because that was what he understood. Needless to say, I found a good deal of this right up there with transposing census tracts.

That summer I got a job as a scrub nurse at Parkland Hospital, Southwestern's teaching facility. A scrub nurse is a sort of operating room technician. Gowned and gloved like the surgeons, the scrub nurse manages all their materials and instruments for them, keeping track of sutures and sponges, slapping scalpels and probes into the doctors' hands, just like on television.

Parkland's most famous emergency surgical patient had been President Kennedy. When I arrived six years later, I discovered that the hospital emergency room had a very active knife and gun club; individuals, couples and families on Friday and Saturday nights would bring their blankets and picnic baskets to a hill in front of the ER entrance, where they'd settle down to watch the evening's casualties hauled in.

It was quite a show.

Inside, I pulled a lot of double shifts that summer, and got to see some amazing stuff myself. ER surgery is medicine on the fly. It was not at all uncommon to be sitting around throwing cards in a hat when, *blam!* the double doors would fly open. "We've got somebody *now!*" an EMT would shout, pushing a bloody mass our way.

The surgeon—in the Parkland ER they were all second-year surgery residents—would just start opening up the patient. You'd build the room from there, adding more personnel and equipment if the guy didn't die right away. Most of the time, he didn't last more than a couple of minutes.

Once, they brought in a half-drunk gunshot victim. He basically was bleeding to death, but he wouldn't give permission to operate. As long as a patient was of sound mind, more or less, you could not open him up against his wishes.

So the surgeon did what anyone would do in such a situation: He ordered a pizza. He said, "When the pizza's delivered, turn off this guy's IVs." So the pizza came and they flipped off the IVs. It took about twenty minutes for the guy to become sufficiently shocky that he no longer was of sound mind, and we could proceed to do whatever we thought was necessary.

In my second year at Southwestern I was fortunate enough to discover a specialty, pathology, that ideally suited my strengths and interests—and a professor who made the subject fascinating for me: Dr. Bruce Fallis.

The pathologist deals directly with diseased tissue, usually under a microscope, but not necessarily. Most other physicians do not. They see reflections of the disease in symptoms or maybe X rays or perhaps changes in body chemistry. But in pathology you see the disease itself. You hold it in your hands. You look directly at it through a microscope. That appealed to me; I liked the exactness.

Being a pathologist also means you don't see trivial stuff. No colds or sniffles or well-baby physicals, only diseases of consequence. And you see all the diseases in all different parts of the body. You see everything that is common, and you see everything that is rare. And you never learn it all.

The stereotype of the pathologist is the weird duck. Some people go into pathology because they cannot handle human contact. They retreat into pathology, as opposed to choosing it. A lot of them are nerdy. However, the ones I trained with were fairly normal.

Our guiding light was Dr. Fallis, a tremendous teacher whom we all held in the greatest awe, me more than most. Fallis was a no-nonsense guy. He looked like a marine corps drill sergeant, and browbeat his students in the finest boot-camp tradition.

Each of us was held to uncompromising standards. His only acceptable level of performance was perfect. You could not *not* know everything about a case. I had never before encountered an instructor such as him.

After my second year I did a summer rotation on the autopsy service at Parkland. My classmate Charlie Cramer, now my partner in practice, shared the job with me. We were given some instruction in how to conduct an autopsy and get all your body parts in different piles. After completing an autopsy one morning, you had until seven the next morning, when you presented the case to your professor. That meant that once you thought you'd figured out what had happened to the deceased, you went to the medical library and worked nearly nonstop for almost twenty-four hours trying to learn as much as you could about what you *thought* had gone on. We all knew that Fallis would grill us to the point of humiliation if we weren't prepared.

My very first case was a young man who'd died while cleaning a petroleum tank. The vessel had not been properly ventilated, and he'd been overwhelmed. He died in the ICU on oxygen therapy.

Now, I had practically memorized Dr. Fallis's textbook; I had read it four or five times. But damn my luck, the disease I had seen in the autopsy room was not described there. So now I had to present a full medical history, which I'd never seen done, about a disease I couldn't identify.

Next morning at seven, my knees knocking, I suggested bilobar pneumococcal pneumonia.

"In twenty years of medicine," Fallis sardonically observed when I finished, "I've never heard a more inept, ill-prepared presentation. I'm extremely disappointed. Maybe we can go through this and clarify it."

That was the high point of the morning. Over the next three and a half hours, I would be asked every question a human can ask. When Fallis was done, and I sat whimpering in the corner, he explained that my cadaver had died of oxygen toxicity pneumonitis, which means the level of pure oxygen needed to keep him alive in the ICU had killed him. Since I'd never heard of such a condition, it was tough to read up on it.

Thirteen

Peach:
The women in my family are well accustomed to domestic catastrophes.

Both my grandmothers lost their husbands to sudden deaths. My father died of radiation sickness.

My mother, Edna Howard of Griffin, Georgia, met Lawrence Olson in the late 1930s at a state experimental farm not far from Griffin (the postmark was, and is, Experiment, Georgia). Edna was a library assistant; Lawrence was an agronomist down from Illinois. During this period, he did research in several labs, including the government's atomic energy facility at Oak Ridge, Tennessee.

I hardly recall my father. He had suffered radiation exposure at Oak Ridge, and would die a lingering death in 1951. Mother, then forty-one, had me to support, along with my two older brothers: Howard, who was born in 1941, and Wayne, who came along in 1944. She continued working as a librarian, taught classes and attended night school at Emory, where she received her master's degree. There was zero money in the house, but I didn't once hear her complain.

Ever practical, she suggested that my recently widowed Grandmother Olson come to live with us. Alice Olson would tell me on repeated occasions that when her husband, Carl, died, she had no will to go on living. Coming to help out her daughter-in-law, however, had given Alice a second life, a reason to go on. Still, hardly a day passed until her death in 1980 when she didn't say, "I sure miss that old Swede of mine."

Mother saw her role as our provider. She worked extremely hard and was always gone. She figured that as long as she provided for us, she was doing what was necessary. To this day, she'll say she did it "for you children."

Beck is not unlike my mother in that way. Both are models of practical self-sufficiency.

She certainly would hug me and tell me that she loved me. But the person who brushed and braided my hair in the morning, and made sure I finished my oatmeal, was my grandmother.

Alice and I slept together in the same room, with me on the rollaway bed, for as long as I can remember. During the day, she kept herself active doing everything from organizing postcards to looking at picture books with me. She did whatever she could without stepping on my mother's toes. She always deferred to Edna—probably the only way these two strong-willed women were going to get along under the same roof.

Big brother Howard—we always called him Howie—was my surrogate father, an essential figure in my girlhood, my adult life and the story of my family. He is key to understanding Beck and me.

With my mother away most of the time, someone had to drive me to Girl Scout meetings and school functions and otherwise take a hand in guiding my development. Howie did that. I clearly remember showing Howie my report card, where I made all *A*'s. He said, "Why didn't you make *A*-pluses?" I was crushed.

Early on in my relationship with Peach, I was somewhat competitive with Howard, simply because he was awfully bright and capable. Whenever I'm around somebody like that, I tend to try to compete with him. I enjoy the give-and-take. Peach noticed that and suggested I stop it, and I did. Howard was too kind to correct me. I grew to love him as a brother.

Peach:

I realize this upbringing left me incomplete. A child needs two parents.

Yet it did put starch in my spine. I think my mother, so competent and hardworking and focused on our material well-being, effectively deleted the word *quit* from my vocabulary. Whatever my situation, particularly my marriage, I make it work. In an odd way, she may also have predisposed me to accept Beck and his own single-minded pursuit of goals, so similar to hers. I certainly had no model at home of what a good marriage should be. As a result, when things later started going bad with Beck, I would think, Who knows? Maybe this is the way they all are.

I was born in late August, which meant that I always was the youngest one in my class, a disadvantage I made sure not to repeat when our daughter Meg also was born in late August. Meg didn't start kindergarten until after her sixth birthday.

I made great grades but was a late bloomer socially, real quiet and shy. I don't think I had a lot of self-assurance. That didn't mean I avoided social situations, but I didn't get much out of them, either. I'd go out with somebody and afterward just think, Yecch! One time, a guy I didn't even know asked me to marry him. That certainly puzzled me. I remembered wondering what love really was. I was clueless.

My mother absolutely drove my brothers to attend the best colleges possible. Howie, who was very bright, took an undergraduate degree at Princeton, his master's at the Georgia Institute of Technology, and earned a doctorate in textile physics at the University of Manchester in England. He'd later design the fabric for a NASA space suit.

Wayne attended the University of Georgia. When it came to me, Edna said, "You don't know what you're going to do; why don't you go to the University of Georgia and become a teacher? That would fit in nicely with having a family."

I wasn't consumed with either prospect. If anything was on my mind, it was a growing sense that I'd led a much too circumscribed life, that I really needed to get out of Griffin and see something of the world.

After graduating from Griffin High School, I went to the University of Georgia, where I took an undergraduate degree in political science in 1971. I then took enough courses to be certified as a resource teacher for gifted children, which is what I was doing in 1974 when Beck and I first met.

The first real go-steady romance of my life was Martha Moyer, whom I met in my sophomore year at Midwestern. She was a beautiful girl with a kind spirit and upbeat manner. What made Martha truly special, however, was that she thought I hung the moon. She could see beyond my nerdiness, past the insecurities, and we connected.

We stayed together through graduation. Then, when I entered Southwestern, Martha moved to Dallas to teach school. The question of marriage arose, but with the extraordinary demands I knew that eight years of medical training would make on me, I wasn't ready for the added responsibility of being a husband, too. Martha moved on, and I'm sure she's glad she did.

I met Margaret Olson, one of my brother Kit's patients, in 1974 on a trip home to Griffin. Kit's wife warned me about Margaret. "I'm not sure about this, Beck," she said. "Margaret's the kind of gal you wind up marrying."

Margaret Olson was just as pretty as she could be, and very bright, very articulate. She has this quality of being a really good person, and that appealed to me. It wasn't just knowing right from wrong. She has a sensitivity to other people that I don't possess. At some level, I could see myself standing next to this person for a lifetime, the mother of my children.

Peach:

I really don't remember our first date. I think we went to Underground Atlanta and probably had dinner or something. But I do remember what I wore: navy-blue hose and a two-piece dress with navy-blue knit sleeves. It was sort of red, white and blue in an argyle pattern. It just gives me the chills to think I once dressed like that.

I recall a strong sense of Beck's energy from that date, but no sparks between us. Maybe six months later, Jane called me again to say that Beck was coming to town once more and would like to see me. Just like him to delegate the date making.

The occasion was to be Kit Weathers's Georgia Jamboree Show of Shows, a weekend dance where Kit and his band played in an old one-room elementary school in Griffin. Kit had purchased the place so his band would have somewhere to play. I discovered that Beck was a good dancer. After someone handed me a beer—I'm a cheap drunk—I started dancing like I'd never danced before. We danced all night.

Beck said, "I'll call you," and did—every Saturday night at some crazy hour, like two in the morning. Then I'd start waking up at two, waiting for his call. Beck was interesting. He made me laugh. He was never dull. He was always a little elusive, a challenge. He made me think. He was different.

It would be years before I finally understood that he talks a lot but never says anything about himself. It takes a while to figure that out.

My medical school buddies at first referred to my future wife as the Georgia Peach. Later, it was G. Peach. And then just Peach. Thus another perfectly good Southern name was lost.

Peach:

At the time, I didn't mind the nicknames at all. It was done in good humor and with affection.

Later on, however, when my marriage began falling apart, it bothered me quite a lot. I'd lost *both* my first and last names. Margaret Olson had disappeared.

On my first visit to Dallas, my mother suggested that I read a number of current periodicals and do abstracts from them on three-by-five cards to cue myself on world events, in order to be an interesting dinner partner for Beck. I'm sure she meant well.

Beck and I exchanged three or four visits through 1974, and then I decided to move to Dallas, where I taught for a year at a local private school. I kept my own address, naturally. I'm that kind of Southern girl. Beck was certainly the reason I went to Texas. But whether that was a tangible gesture of love, I don't know. I really wanted to get out of Griffin. I thought I loved him, though. I thought I was absolutely in love with him.

When I finished my residency, I was offered a fellowship in Boston. When I told Peach, she said, "Well, chief, I ain't moving to Boston unless some decisions are made. That's the way it is."

Peach:

I told him I wasn't going to Boston with him unless we were married. At first, I was devastated that it required such an ultimatum to make him think. Then I was angry with him. Then I was simply certain my stance was correct. He took a weekend to think it over.

If she had not made marriage an issue, I would have been happy just to live with her in Boston. It wasn't that I didn't love her. But actually coming to grips with the concept of being married was a challenge. Eventually, I did conclude that I was a whole lot better off with her than without her. I loved her. But I really didn't have a clue. It amazed me that I had just taken eight years preparing to start my career, and here I was ready to take at least as big a step with no real preparation whatsoever.

Fourteen

Peach:

He never really proposed. He just came back and said, "I can't live without you." I think we got married because I was standing in the right place at the right time. That's not so unusual. I think it happens with a lot of guys.

At age twenty-six, I was still a girl in many ways, with some Pollyannaish ideas. From that standpoint, we probably were a decent match. He was not real sophisticated emotionally, either. We were both very naive.

Our wedding was April 24, 1976, at the First Baptist Church. It was a big affair, with four hundred guests, the sort of moment you live for in Griffin. There was no engagement ring, which really didn't bother me. I used my grandmother's ring for my wedding ring and I purchased Beck's for him at a discount jeweler's in Dallas. If I hadn't been so in love, I would have realized that the $1,200's worth of camera equipment he'd just bought himself would have bought a nice little diamond.

As it turned out, Beck wore his band only on rare, formal occasions. He told me the reason was that he feared getting the ring caught in something, causing injury or, even worse, the loss of a finger.

Beck also had neglected to get us a hotel room for our wedding night, so we stayed at his parents' house in Atlanta. That should have told me something.

The next day, we packed up and drove off for Boston. Our local newspaper, ever eager to report events in the best possible light, informed readers that our honeymoon would consist of "a leisurely drive up the Atlantic seaboard."

I rarely had been outside Georgia. Besides vacation trips to Florida and the year I lived in Dallas, I had visited Chicago and New Orleans, and traveled with my mother and Wayne to New Jersey to watch Howie graduate from Princeton. That was it.

Beck may have been better traveled than I, but he, too, had severely limited horizons. These included an untutored palate. I discovered, for example, that he did not eat fish. The good news was that once I got him started, he'd try anything.

When we first got to Boston I brought up my interest in finding a teaching job. But positions weren't plentiful in the local private schools, and they didn't pay much. Plus, there were lots of couples like us, which meant competition for every available job. Once we compared my likely pay with the cost of commuting and other expenses, it was practically a wash.

Still, I felt a need to justify my day. If he was putting in long hours, then I would, too. It had to do with my self-esteem. I had to be busy to make it look like I was earning my keep.

I did some volunteer work at the hospital, and helped Beck assemble his professional research library. This consisted mostly of typing his notes. I was pretty isolated, but I really didn't mind that. I like being by myself, and had spent a lot of time alone as a girl.

I love Boston, and I loved where we lived, a third-floor apartment in a row house on Longwood Avenue. That place had a lot of personality. I was also able to walk to work, which I liked. Michael Dukakis, then governor of Massachusetts, didn't live far away, and sometimes I'd run into him on his way to the MTA.

I was not so excited by my work. I was the junior guy, and I soon figured out that all they wanted was a gofer. I ended up doing the autopsies no one else felt like doing, or covering when no one else wanted to work. That included the bicentennial celebration weekend in 1976 when the tall ships came in. Peach and I were on our way out the door when the phone rang.

"Guess what, fella. You're it."

I spent the entire weekend locked in the morgue, reviewing cases.

Peach:

It took me a while to figure out that Beck probably was depressed when we married—and he remained depressed, more or less, from then on. I had never been around a depressed person. I didn't know what it meant when he'd complain about this hurt or that hurt and would go to bed. I knew he had a lot of trouble sharing feelings, but I took comfort in the fact that he was that way with everyone, not just me. At first I thought it would just fade away. If he learns to trust, I'd think. If he learns that no matter what, I'm here. But it never happened.

I felt I needed to be working all the time. I'm not equipped to relax and enjoy myself. It is awfully hard on anyone around you if you are not a happy person, and that's been pretty steady throughout my life.

But here's something else. I admire Peach's emphasis on interpersonal communication. I regard it as one of her strengths. I just have a great deal of trouble emulating her. It is not that I don't care to do the right thing, or make the appropriate gesture, or say the correct words. I just do not naturally think of it. Never occurs to me. This is an inadvertent part of why I have disappointed and angered Peach so often, and possibly one reason I so often misread her, which I have repeatedly done over the years.

Peach:

Boston was supposed to be the beginning of intimacy. Instead it was the beginning of distance. I thought I was to blame. I was not a brilliant conversationalist, certainly not in realms that Beck would consider interesting. My mother made sure I didn't forget that.

I did try to talk to him, but he always shut it down. And I felt he was so much smarter than I that I was intimidated. That was not entirely his fault.

"How was your day?" certainly never got me anywhere. "How were the brain tumors?" wasn't going to work either.

One of the reasons I can seem uncommunicative to Peach is that I often have something technical on my mind that I doubt would interest her: "Dear, isn't it interesting how a GPS satellite works?"

I know she wants to engage more in "How are you feeling? What is going through your mind right now?" Usually, there's a big goose egg sitting there. I think she sometimes gives me too much credit for actually having thoughts.

Peach:

I'd later learn something else about Beck. He has this strong need not to be answerable, to be independent. He believed all women are controlling, by their very nature.

As for me, I didn't have anything with which to compare my

marriage. I was not unhappy, and Beck at his best is gentle, generous and undemanding. He's no autocrat. So for the time being I decided to be content that I'd married a good man who was a good provider—and just hoped that he was steady. The truth is, if you're looking for someone intuitive and sensitive, marry a woman.

Fifteen

Much as we liked Boston, I was pleasantly surprised one day to hear from Tom Dickey, a fellow pathologist who'd completed his residency with me at Southwestern. Tom was also a good friend; he and his wife had hosted an engagement party for Peach and me.

Dickey and several other highly capable young pathologists I knew from my days at Southwestern had formed a partnership in Dallas with Jim Ketchersid, whom I knew by reputation to be both a fine doctor and an incredibly honorable guy. Jim has an unwavering instinct for doing the right thing. When Dickey invited me to join their partnership, I accepted without hesitation.

"Don't you want to know how much we're going to pay you?" Tom asked when I didn't.

"Not really," I answered.

"C'mon."

"I figure you guys will pay me what my services are worth at the point they are worth something."

I had complete and well-placed faith in my new partners.

April of 1977, Peach and I returned to Dallas, where I went to work at Medical City Hospital (then more of a village than a city), a three-year-old facility with approximately one hundred beds that soon would morph into a huge complex. It was built on prairie land far enough north of downtown that during dove season, staffers could saunter out just past the parking lot to blast away on their lunch hour.

Medicine demands a lot of your time. But I had made a reasonable attempt to stay fit, largely by running, which is cheap, doesn't require much more than a set of sneakers and can be done anywhere.

During our year in Boston, I ran thirty to forty miles a week, but never in races. I just liked to run.

When we moved back to Dallas we lived for a year in a house not far from Medical City, and I'd often jog to and from work, about six miles. It was a fairly easy way to force myself to get a little exercise. I certainly did not have an image of myself as an athlete. I just liked to be fit.

But gradually I realized I was in pretty good shape. There was even the gratification of discovering people less than half my age, *athletes,* who couldn't do what I did. These were the high school football players I encountered toward the end of my first summer back in Dallas. We shared the same running track, and I was delighted at every chance to run right around them, as if they were standing still, dying. It was one of my life's great pleasures.

Peach:

When we got back to Texas and Beck started working really long hours I did get lonely, and lonelier and lonelier. I started thinking about having children. This was not out of a strong maternal instinct. I had spent very little time around kids, and frankly had been a disaster as a baby-sitter. I am very squeamish, cannot stand the sight of blood, even my own, even on television.

Yet I really wanted to have a child, and so decided on my own that we would. I didn't actually stop taking the Pill, as Beck has suspected. But I did sort of play Russian roulette. The result was our son, Beck, who was born in October 1978.

I was knocked flat. I didn't know anything about marriage, but what I didn't know about marriage paled in comparison with what I didn't know about parenthood. Getting used to the idea was a big hurdle, like moving tectonic plates.

Peach:

Beck was not crazy about helping me out. But it was very fulfilling for me to have that little boy *demanding* my love and attention. I threw all my energy into him, which made me a happier person. Beck was throwing all his energy into work, so it allowed us to coexist better, I think.

This was also the time that I started making connections with other women, most of them young mothers like myself, who later would become my indispensable circle of confidantes.

The first one I met was Pat White, whose husband, Terry, practices at Medical City with Beck. Pat and I met when we were both pregnant with our first children, at a holiday house party for the Medical City staff. By coincidence, her son, Charles, and my Bub were seated together at Meadowbrook preschool in North Dallas (both their last names begin with W) and began a friendship that has endured all the way into college. Charles and Beck were roommates for their first two years at Duke.

Another early acquaintance was Cecilia Boone. The Boones' daughter, Aimee, attended Meadowbrook, too. Cecilia and I met when she invited me to join her carpool. Later, when the Boones bought a house near ours, their second child, Katherine, and our Meggie became—and remain—as inseparable as Bub and Charles White.

Beck at Windy Corner, Mt. McKinley, 1989.

PART THREE

Sixteen

If you've never felt very good about yourself, you never really expect to, and therefore you don't begrudge your lack of happiness. You're never content, but you manage.

That is not to say you function normally. You are not emotionally whole, and you cannot bring much value to your personal relationships. But you can keep putting one foot in front of the other, day in and day out, just as you must do when you climb mountains. There's even a certain grim satisfaction in succeeding in this way, by sheer dint of will and intelligence.

That was my outlook in the early years of my marriage. I did what I've always done best—work—and I courted a sufficient number of challenges and diversions to keep my mind engaged. It was a form of running away, of course.

I tend to be a little over the top at first with a new idea or interest. I'll get fascinated and learn a lot about it. Then having scratched that itch, I move on to something else.

My first hobby was a Hobie; that is, a Hobie Cat, a type of

small sailboat in which I navigated Dallas-area lakes during my residency at Southwestern. This was not a fleeting interest. My long-term goal was to sail around the world. The cat was simply a first step in what I expected would be a methodical, protracted process leading to the actual expedition. Events, however, intervened.

I took correspondence courses in every imaginable subject, from oceanography to marine meteorology, acquiring as much technical knowledge and sailing skill as one can living several hundred miles from the nearest saltwater. I also attended sailing schools and assembled a large sailing library. Some of my practical experience was gained in the Caribbean, where I went "bareboating"—renting a boat with no captain or crew—on a couple of occasions.

If you think you're good at shading the truth, you ought to see what it takes to convince some guy he should rent you, a stranger, his valuable sailboat for a few days. The first time I went I took along Tom Dickey and his then-wife, who was dubious enough to commit her last will and testament to toilet paper on the flight down from Dallas.

I instructed them not to ask any questions in front of the boat's owner, just to stand there and look knowledgeable. If they were to inquire what the front and back are called, I explained, or what that tall thing in the center was, we might end up nailed to the dock, or drinking mai tais someplace, but we definitely would not be sailing.

Dickey called me Captain Bligh.

On my second bareboating excursion, I took along my father, my brother Dan, Tom Dickey, and my brother-in-law Howard, who would be the team cook. Once again I had to warn this band of lubbers—Howie had done some sailing—not to betray their inexperience until we were safely away.

Sailing was a parallel to my later mountain climbing in that it involved the serious pursuit over time of the skills I thought I'd eventually need to achieve a somewhat unrealistic goal way off in the future. Gradually, I raised the bar. On the first trip we rented a thirty-two-and-a-half footer, for example. The second time the boat was a fairly sophisticated forty-one-footer. It was also like training to become a doctor, a matter of taking apart a chore and defining all the little baby steps that will get you where you want to go. Along the way, I picked up a succession of licenses and certificates, little trophies to mark my progress, substantive official proof of achievement, like merit badges or that God and Country Award I earned in Saudi Arabia but never received.

Out of sailing there also grew a second pastime—ham radio. This avocation lasted about two years. I enjoyed learning it, and I kept collecting ever higher licenses until I hit the top rank, which is called ham extra. By then I'd erected a one-hundred-foot radio tower in our side yard.

The professional portion of my life—the part to which I devoted so much time and energy—blossomed nicely. Unlike other physicians, who build practices over time, my group has a large and reliable clientele, the patient population at Medical City, whom we attend under contract with the hospital. Month to month, we serve at the hospital's pleasure.

In 1982, I was elected president of the twelve-hundred person medical staff at Medical City, a three-year commitment:

one year as president-elect, one as president and one as past president. At age thirty-five, I was easily the youngest person ever elected to the job. I spent my term in office employing the sorts of political and organizational skills few medical doctors are ever called upon to exercise. I discovered I had a gift for leading large organizations, that I can mold opinion and understand the logic of an impending struggle, no matter what's being said. I also am not easily dissuaded.

One other obvious benefit of the job, when you work as a franchise as we do, is that your livelihood is unlikely to be taken away when you're chief of staff.

I enjoyed it although—or perhaps because—my institutional and professional responsibilities were huge and unrelenting and tended to elbow aside competing claims on my time, particularly those of my wife and children.

Domestic life was not my forte. I wasn't good at it—at all.

"All this work is for us," I'd say to Peach. Whether that was or was not true, it made a good line.

My material success gave me something to hide behind, too. You certainly think that if you're working really hard and you're bringing home the bacon, and you give your family the things they want, that's a big chunk of what you, as a man, are supposed to provide. I could say to myself, How bad can I be? I work hard. I provide all these things. I love them.

I would learn that loving someone, even loving them so hard your teeth hurt, is necessary, but not sufficient if you are not there for them. If you're not there when they need you, then you force them to make a life without you. They have no other choice. You may believe that at some point you can turn around and say, "Now, I'm ready." But you'll only discover that they've moved on. At some point you're going to wind up a lonely old man, surrounded by your things.

It is possible that the hard work in the early 1980s had one other tonic effect, albeit a hidden one. Besides providing Peach and the children with creature comforts and financial security, as well as securing my own professional status, my three years as a doctor/administrator may have forestalled the return of my depression. I have no scientific evidence that this is so. But I can report that after my three-year commitment drew to a close, I rapidly decompressed.

Studies seem to show that those of us who believe we must achieve in order to merit love and respect—not just be ourselves—are vulnerable to emotional troughs when our opportunities to excel are restricted.

Terry White:

I have known Beck Weathers since he first came to the hospital. He is both a friend and colleague and our families are very close.

My routine is to visit with a pathologist, looking at the tissue slides, before I go see a patient. As a result, I see Beck a good deal, four or five times a week.

The mark of the good pathologist is wanting to know critical information about the patient, so that it helps him, or her, to provide relevant information in turn. Beck is excellent at that. We have a give-and-take relationship, which is professionally very rewarding.

Beck's attractive qualities include his confidence. We build on mutual respect in our profession. And he's obviously a talker. Beck could talk the paint off a wall.

Pat White:

Terry and Beck are like a couple of nerds. They like to get together over a double microscope and look at slides of Terry's patients and solve difficult problems together. They've always been friends.

Terry White:

Beck has keen insights, and an incisive approach to issues and problems, which we took advantage of when he was president of the medical staff. He's a problem solver and a consensus builder. Beck can convince people that his point of view is valid. And he's flexible enough to know there is more than one way of looking at things.

I recently was president of the medical staff myself, and I know that the job is really involving. It easily consumes a third of your time. Then it's over. You're no longer the person that everyone looks to for leadership and decisions. There can be a real letdown.

I missed the interplay of agendas and personalities, and the decision making. I got a lot of feedback as president, and most of it was very positive. I felt affirmed. When suddenly I was no longer engaged, full throttle, all the time, the black dog crawled back into my life. A brutal chapter was about to begin.

Depression does not overwhelm you in a day. It's very gradual. At first you might just feel blue, or not zippedy-doo-dah. You don't pay much attention to it. You think to yourself, Well, everybody has down days. You can't be up all the time. Basically, you just try to ignore it, expecting it to go away.

But it gets worse and worse, and you realize at some point, This has gone past not feeling up. After about six months, I was fairly miserable. There was no apparent cause for this. It just felt as if I'd stepped into a black hole.

It's a complete coincidence that just as this second depression hit I also discovered mountaineering. Actually, I had received a foretaste of its seductions some years earlier.

Hiking never interested me as an adult, and I didn't give it much thought until around 1980 when Peach and I went on a backpacking expedition to Texas's Big Bend National Park with some other doctors and their families. This is beautiful countryside, full of wonderful vistas, but it is also arid and hot, a climate dominated by the Chihuahua Desert across the Rio Grande in Mexico.

About halfway through our hike I was incredibly dry, could have peed dust. My canteen was long since drained, and I'd annihilated the single apple I'd been given. So this gal in front of me starts nibbling her apple in slow motion. I watched her in an agonal state, pretty much like a dog at table. When she got ready to throw the core away, I asked her for it and grabbed it and sucked it right down to the seeds. Then I looked around and announced that I was heading back the way we came. The only thing on my mind was my thirst.

I ran the six miles or so back to our van, where I knew there was a big ice chest full of cold beer in the back. When I got there, I opened six cans at once, set them all up on the hood, and addressed each in turn. One by one, I knocked them down. By the time I got to the end I was just beginning to feel perhaps I wasn't going to die on the spot.

Dehydration aside, I had a great time on this outing. I enjoyed being out in nature with the pretty views, as well as the camaraderie. It was a lot of fun.

Now fast-forward to 1985 and the very earliest stages of my depression. On another group holiday, this time at the YMCA camp in Estes Park, Colorado, all the dads decide to get up early one morning for an eight-mile hike. However, next morning, a freezing rain is falling. It's really cold and nasty. Only two of us, myself and Ken Zornes, whom Peach and I had met through the Boones, show up in the gloom. Every other cabin is pitch black.

Garrett Boone:

Cecilia and I were the ones who pulled together that Y-camp group. I remember Beck and Ken Zornes invited me along on their morning hike. I said I'd think about it. I heard the gravel crunch as they drove up. That's when I pulled the pillow over my head and went back to sleep.

We headed up the trail anyway, and came marching back hours later just *filled* with ourselves for being so bold and determined and manly to complete the hike while everyone else—the sane ones—stayed in bed.

Estes Park became an annual summer event, and cemented a sort of Mutt and Jeff relationship between us.

Ken and I are nothing alike. He is tall and a real jock and supremely confident of his physical gifts. There never is any question in Ken's mind that his body can do anything. He just takes a look at something and says, "Boy, that'd be fun to do."

My self-image wasn't athletic at all. Although I jogged or walked to work each day and otherwise kept myself fit, my innate self-doubt and the shadow slowly smothering my spirit made me cautious. We'd look at a peak. He'd say, "Let's go for it!" I'd say, "Maybe we ought to try something a little more rational."

Ken Zornes:

Most people don't want to get up at three o'clock and go out and punish themselves for twelve hours. But we did. Either it's in you or it isn't. I remember I broke an artery in my finger on a rock climb one time. We just laughed our asses off about that. Kept asking each other, "Are you having fun yet?"

We were like the tortoise and the hare. When we'd cross a boulder field on hikes, for instance, Beck went ahead methodically, putting one foot in front of the other. I'd run forty yards and then stop with my tongue hanging out. Here comes Beck. About the time he gets to me, I take off again. We both get to the top about the same time, just different styles of getting there.

We could hike for hours and not say a word. When we did talk, usually it was Beck who talked and I listened. That's also part of what made us a good team. I don't talk a whole lot, and he does.

Usually we would go for it, really pushing ourselves on these trips. Each year we'd get up there and try to find something challenging. One time, for instance, we climbed three contiguous peaks in one day. That was pretty tiring.

We also managed to make some very big mistakes that we were lucky to survive. One was the decision to save ourselves a long walk by sliding down this glacier on plastic garbage bags. My only other equipment was a walking stick with a small metal point. We made it down uninjured, too ignorant to realize how narrowly we'd cheated death, how easily we might have accelerated down that glacier to oblivion, just as the feckless Chen Yu-Nan later would on Everest.

Garrett Boone:

To show you how far Beck traveled on his quest, on our first trip to Estes Park I went on an overnight hike with Ken Zornes, Ken's son, Ben, Beck and little Beck. We got to where we wanted to camp and set up the tents. The boys amused themselves with a pissing contest off a rock, seeing how far they could shoot it.

Beck surprised me by unpacking a six-pack of beer. That seemed the most important thing to him about this hike. He got to the top with a six-pack.

Ken Zornes:

One of our earliest hikes was up a mountain called Flat Top. It was a beautiful twelve-thousand-footer. Suddenly a storm came in. I think we had windbreakers and sandwiches with us. It got really cold and snowy. We hunkered down shoulder to shoulder against some rocks, because we couldn't see the trail to get back down.

I remember us saying, "What the hell are we going to do? Die here?"

Fortunately, after about twenty minutes the storm moved on. The sun came out and we took off for another peak. But we did learn. We never went up there again without plenty of gear.

We were definitely summer soldiers, but gradually, by trial and error, Ken and I did learn a few basic lessons about mountaineering.

The year after that first climb, I went to Alaska with Jim Ketchersid and a group of other doctors to hike the Chilkoot Trail, a storied thirty-three-mile track that leads up from Skagway to 3,525-foot Chilkoot Pass and then into the Canadian Yukon. Tens of thousands of so-called stampeders took the same rugged trail in search of their fortunes during the Alaskan gold rush of a hundred years ago. I had a great time chugging along through forests and swamps and past old tin cans, bottles, stoves and even boats discarded by the prospectors.

The Chilkoot trek also confirmed a surprise discovery I'd made about climbing: The strenuous, focused exertion out in the mountain wilds relieved my deepening depression, if only for a while. I could throw off the gloom out there, because mountains—particularly big mountains, as I would learn—

force you to be in the moment. You're absorbed by your labors and by your surroundings, physically and emotionally liberated from the world below. It became a form of self-medication.

Cecilia Boone:

As Beck and Ken got more and more involved in climbing on *family* vacations, all of us were very much aware of it. The whole thing was oriented toward family, but Beck and Ken either were not there at all, or were exhausted. This was a family vacation for everyone but them. They had their own agenda. Both Peach and Debbie Zornes were irritated, at best.

By this time, around 1987, the black dog was my constant companion, and I was to some extent trapped with him by my absolute unwillingness to admit my condition and to seek professional help. My motive, by the way, wasn't so much to hide the truth from others as it was to deny it to myself. I could not admit that I suffered such a weakness.

I was further isolated by my deep distrust of psychiatry and a practical abhorrence of medication. I don't necessarily think of psychologists and psychiatrists as mountebanks and fools, but that's close to what I believe. I am a very concrete person; what they do strikes me as mumbo jumbo. I simply couldn't believe that just talking to someone was going to make a difference.

As a doctor, I also worried about jeopardizing my professional standing by admitting I was depressed, that there was something medically wrong with me. I certainly did not want someone determining whether I was fit to practice. I was not going to regularly report to someone to demonstrate that I was okay.

I really wasn't okay.

I was overcome with deep, deep sadness and hopelessness. It was like looking down into a dark well, not knowing how in the world I was going to get out. It seemed so much stronger than me.

At work I was having a horrible time with my concentration. Half the time I was reading out my surgical cases, I was thinking of how pleasant it would be if the pain would stop—and I knew an easy way to do that.

Of course, I'd been miserable when the first depression descended over me in college, but then at least I could go lie down for three or four hours. Now I had to be upright, and upbeat, especially at work. I couldn't let *any* of it show.

So with no outlet at work, it became even harder to keep it together at home. Sometimes I'd come home and only make it as far as the garage door before I'd have to sit down for five minutes, trying to get myself back together enough to walk in the house.

As before, there was a lot of ideation about ending it all, the kind of thing where you go to the bookstore in search of the manual on how to kill yourself. You don't want to screw it up. The ideal way seemed to be a really good bottle of scotch and a large amount of pills. Then I decided that avenue required too many proactive steps. I began to think that if it really came down to it, I'd probably try something a little messier.

The absolute lowest point, where I really scared myself, came one night while I was sitting on the sofa, holding my .357, and thinking this was a good time to drive out to the lake. The inner certainty I'd felt about suicide seemed about to express itself in action. I felt there really was no other solution, no place to turn, no refuge, except the mountains.

Seventeen

Peach:

I knew that Beck was in pain.

At first I asked myself, What have I done? What can I do? I blamed myself for it. For a long time I believed I'd failed him. And I'd failed myself. Growing up without a father, all I ever wanted was for *my* children to have a father.

Not until much later did I finally understand that this wasn't my fault. All I knew at the time was that I could have packed up and left with the children, and Beck would not have noticed until the house payment came due.

I tried everything I could think of to get his attention. Affection and attention. That didn't work. Withholding affection and attention. That didn't work. Finally I decided to be the best doctor's wife I could be, and just wait and see if he grew out of it. Wait for him to change. It's just a period, I told myself. All guys go through phases. Then I thought, Maybe this is a *long* phase.

Bub:

I've never doubted that my father loves me. I didn't always agree with how he spent his time.

Meg:

I remember when I was really young and he was driving me to school, I said, "Daddy, promise me you'll never climb Mount Everest."

He said, "Okay." I don't think he was as obsessed then as he got later.

When we were young, Mom was *always* there. Dad was there sometimes. I pined for his attention. All I wanted him to do was be around. It's not that I didn't value my mother just as much. I did, and I do. It's just that she was always reliably there, so I didn't *have* to pine for her.

Ken and I harbored an ambition to climb Longs Peak, a 14,255-foot mountain northwest of Boulder in Rocky Mountain National Park. The thirty-fifth tallest mountain in the United States, Longs Peak was first climbed in August of 1868 by John Wesley Powell, the explorer and former Union major who'd lost an arm at the battle of Shiloh.

Handicapped as he was, Powell did not attempt Longs Peak via its most famous feature, a sheer, 945-foot-high diamond-shaped rock face known, unsurprisingly, as the Diamond. As famous among rock climbers as El Capitán in Yosemite, the

Diamond is a fearsome natural barrier, especially if you decide to tackle it straight up.

We had no such intention. There's a hiking trail to the top of Longs Peak that would have suited us just fine. However, each July when we came to Estes Park the trail was still closed by the previous winter's snow. Park rangers wouldn't let anyone up there.

We devised an alternative plan. We knew that professional guides took climbers up the Diamond, and that there were routes that even us rank amateurs could negotiate. Thus one bright day on our third or fourth summer at Estes brought me to the highway sign for the Colorado Mountain School, which I previously must have passed a zillion times without ever giving it a thought. As would anyone else so terrified of heights. I don't like steep places at all, never have. If possible, I would have had my crib put on the floor.

Inside I walked, however, and picked up some brochures. After glancing through them with Ken, we decided to take a day of training in rock climbing, a day of ice and snow climbing and then we'd join a so-called technical climb of Longs Peak.

We showed up at the appointed hour for our introductory lesson to discover we were the only students in the class. Both of us were also fairly intimidated by our instructor, Mike Caldwell, a high school wrestling coach about my age who'd been a college gymnast at Berkeley, as well as a bodybuilder. Mike was a former Mr. Colorado. Even his earlobes had muscles.

Ken and I managed to keep our poker faces on as we drove with Mike out to Lumpy Ridge, which is right above Estes Park, and is an excellent rock-climbing area. He started us out with

the basics. "Here is a rope. This is a harness." Then he fa..iil-
iarized us with the Tao of rock climbing, the use of your weight
and balance, not your strength, to climb. In Mike's case, I didn't
see where it mattered. He looked strong enough to pick up and
throw the boulder I was trying to scale.

Of course there are times in rock climbing when you just have
to pump it up and go. But you learn to climb with your feet, not
your hands. A good climber doesn't look up for a handhold, he
looks down for a foot placement. And you need to keep your
weight on top of your feet. It's not realistic to think you are
going to chin yourself up a hill.

Caldwell took us to a boulder about ten feet high to demonstrate some techniques. First was how to get a purchase on the
rock. He pointed out a little crystal jutting perhaps an eighth of
an inch from the surface, like a big button. He put his thumb
over it, then wrapped two fingers over the thumb and pulled
himself up until he could reach the top of the boulder with his
free hand. Then he slowly rolled up onto it. Spiderman is no
defter than that. He made it look like he could do it backward
in his sleep.

We tried it, and pretty soon were more or less flinging ourselves at this rock. Scratched and bleeding, this was our intro-
duction to "red chalk," the mountaineering term for blood
mixed with stone dust.

At one point I saw a bush growing out of the stone and
grabbed it. "This is *rock* climbing," said Mike with a disap-
proving glance. Ashamed, I let go of the plant.

The highlight of the day was to climb a couple of pitches, or
two rope lengths—approximately 160 feet—up a rock face.

Most rock climbing involves installation of wedgelike devices into cracks in the rock. When you pull down on them, these doodads jam tightly and, presumably, are securely wedged. You then attach your rope to them, affording the person behind you a reliable connection to the rock face. If he slips, the wedge will break his fall. It will also keep you from being pulled off the mountain with him.

The rope of choice is mainly nylon, because nylon rope has high elasticity, which helps absorb some of the shock if you fall, sort of like the bungee effect. Nylon also is less likely than stiff line, such as steel cable, to rip out those little devices that keep you attached to the mountain.

The rock face angled up about seventy degrees above us, and the first move required going out over a 150-foot drop. Mike and Ken started up the pitch ahead of me and soon disappeared from view. Standing there by myself, eyeing that first move, I got a little cotton-mouthed. I *hate* heights. Not far away, another group was trying to do more or less what we were doing, but on a much gentler slope. I saw a middle-aged guy, whimpering like a baby, spread-eagle on a deal that looked about as dangerous as an escalator.

Why didn't I get to go over there? I wondered.

But I did move out, and actually managed to get around the overhanging rock. My heart was pounding in my ears. I then started the next move and got about halfway through it when I couldn't find a place to put my feet or anything to grab with my hands. Thirty seconds into my climbing career and suddenly I had the sickening sensation that I was about to head into outer space. Even though Mike had told me I probably was not going to get hurt, and I trusted his word, that really was an act of faith. My body was crying, "Liar, liar, pants on fire!"

Then it happened. I just came peeling off. The wedge above me held, to my abundant relief, and I dangled there for a while, about six or eight inches from the face, until I got myself reattached to the rock and managed to climb up this thing. When I got to the top and told Ken, he was angry that I'd fallen and he didn't. I offered to kick him off the mountain, if he liked.

My major surprise about rock climbing was that while it is the most spectacular type of mountaineering, and can be very challenging physically, it is a pretty safe sport. You may break a few bones but, generally speaking, you are not apt to kill yourself. The obverse of this coin is that snowfield climbing, which looks pretty safe, if arduous, is in fact much more dangerous than rock climbing. Start to slide down one of those little slopes, and you are dead.

Not yet grasping that simple fact, Ken and I headed out the next day for our glacier training. We figured the hard and scary part was behind us. Imagine our amazement, then, when we met a fellow student, a woman, who confided she was deathly afraid of glacier climbing. I was about to reassure her in my manly way that Ken and I already had seen the little thing we were going out to, and that it wasn't steep at all—nothing compared with the rock climbing we'd done yesterday.

Before I could make a fool of myself, however, she let on that she'd just climbed the Petite Grypon, which at that time I knew only from photos in a brochure. But they are all I had to see. The Petite Grypon is incredibly steep, essentially an eight-hundred-foot-tall vertical spire, a needle. I had assumed the only way to get to the top of the thing was with a gun to your head in a helicopter.

Yet this experienced rock climber was telling us she was terrified of going out on that snow, that she'd already taken this particular class twice before. By the end of the day we understood why.

The core of the snow-climbing curriculum is self-arrests, how to stop yourself from skidding away no matter which way you fall—on your face or back, head up or head down. The key lies in correctly deploying your ice ax as a brake.

Mike made a snow bollard—a mound of snow around which he secured a rope—to act as our anchor. Tethered to the bollard, we then practiced the various ways of getting the ax underneath us as we slid, with one hand on the end of the ax and the other down on the shaft, and our weight pressing directly down on it. These were the do's. The single imperative don't was don't ever let your feet dig into the hill. It is a natural instinct to do so. But if you do, and if you are wearing crampons, when they catch on the ice they will likely snap your leg or ankle or, just as bad, launch you into space.

The twenty-mile, approximately sixteen-hour guided climb of Longs Peak began at 2:00 A.M. with a long hike to the bottom of Lamb's Slide, an ice field of about one thousand feet named for Elkanah Lamb, an itinerant preacher who first negotiated the treacherous stretch in 1871. Big rocks routinely rumble down Lamb's Slide. That morning, as I dashed to avoid one of them, I fell flat on my face.

At the top of Lamb's Slide you move onto a traverse that takes you toward the Diamond. Here I encountered my first taste of climber humor. The traverse is called Broadway, which most assuredly it is not. In some places on this trail, there are just a few inches of ledge. For a rookie climber such as myself, deathly afraid of heights, this was not ideal.

When you reach the edge of the Diamond, you then scramble up a relatively easy rock climb, rated 5.4, that takes you to the top, the very apex of the Diamond. At the time, it seemed quite difficult to me, although it's actually a very easy climb. There, you must step from the mountain's east face to its north face to go on, a two- or three-foot affair that would be no big deal except for the fact that you do your little jump over about 2,500 feet of clear air.

I had read about this step with fear and anticipation. Pacing back and forth in my cabin with the brochure, I began to slip around the hardwood floors. I looked down and realized that my feet, like my hands, were sopping with perspiration.

At the moment of truth atop Longs Peak I did not panic—thank goodness—and made my way back down the mountain without incident. It was a transforming moment. I was really frightened up there, yet I'd faced up to that terror and managed to come through it.

That night, a big restaurant dinner was planned for all the families. Ken and I, of course, were whipped, but too macho to admit that. So we got dressed and went to this nice restaurant, where I basically fell asleep, my face planted in the mashed potatoes. I was gone.

Eighteen

Peach:

When we were first dating, but before I moved to Dallas, Beck had the Hobie Cat. Then he got a bigger Hobie Cat. I think I went out once with him.

After he sold it, we crewed with people in Dallas who had a boat. That was fun. I knew his dream was to someday sail around the world in a custom-built boat. That was fine with me. I knew I'd never go because it wouldn't be air-conditioned.

But I did try to share his interest. We took boating lessons together in Fort Myers, Florida. Beck got his captain's license, and I got some sort of certificate too. I thought, Okay, now we can charter a boat over spring break with the kids. But Beck found something else to do instead.

Next came ham radio. It was just a little hobby, and certainly an innocent hobby. I didn't know *how* innocent until later. I don't remember once trying to pull him away from it. But I do recall that after he lost interest I asked if we could take down that tower. The neighbors didn't like it. He said, "Oh, sure."

The trips to Estes Park were fun. What I did not enjoy, however, was being given total responsibility for the kids. This is not a family vacation, I thought.

The one time I remember most clearly, he and Ken got up in the middle of the night to go climb. That evening, we were all going to have our annual meal at a nice restaurant. Beck told me that would be no problem. "Don't worry. We'll be back."

So they came running back in and showered. They were just exhausted, and both of them got drunk in about two seconds.

I was very angry.

Ken Zornes:

I remember very clearly coming back down that day from Longs Peak. We were really pooped. Walking down the trail, I said something about this being really cool.

Beck said, "We need to do more. What's next?"

I said, "Let's go climb McKinley."

Beck said, "Well, okay."

We had a laugh about it. Then we wound up doing that, too.

Mike Caldwell had suggested we try Chimborazo in Ecuador, a 20,702-foot volcano with an interesting distinction: Because the mountain rests on a vast equatorial bulge, Chimborazo's summit actually is the surface point most distant from the center of the planet.

"Why try something simple like that?" Ken said. "Let's go straight to McKinley."

I believe Mike was somewhat skeptical of this hubris. We clearly had no idea what we were getting into.

Mount McKinley, also commonly known as Denali (Athabascan for "high one") is the centerpiece of Denali National Park in Alaska. At 20,320 feet, it is the highest peak in North America and, because it sits so far north of the equator, at 63 degrees latitude, McKinley's weather consistently is the harshest of any big mountain anywhere. Average weather conditions at 14,000 feet on McKinley are the same as at 26,000 feet on Everest.

Winter lows reach ninety-five degrees below zero. Storm gusts have been measured at up 150 miles per hour. It is the biggest mountain on Earth, in terms of mass, and is the tallest in terms of vertical relief, rising eighteen thousand feet above the surrounding lowlands.

More than half the mountain is covered in snowfields, which means you spend a lot of time on snowshoes and skis—otherwise you can't stand up—looking out for crevasses. There is absolutely no finesse involved in climbing McKinley. You do it assault style, same as Everest, which means you must climb it twice, moving your stuff, then following after it. But with no Sherpas handy to tote your gear, it's a lot more work getting to the top.

Denali is also dangerous. Since it was first climbed in 1910, approximately one hundred climbers have died on the mountain. On average, one out of two climbers makes it to the top.

Ken and I, together with two other climbers and a pair of guides from the Colorado Mountain School, would spend three weeks on Denali. In the year leading up to our May 1989 expedition, we took a few more climbing lessons and embarked on a rigorous, if ill-conceived, conditioning program back in Dallas.

We both did some weight training and aerobics, but our principal work was running, about sixty miles a week. We also entered a couple of marathons that year. I managed to constantly injure myself. My shoulders sounded like socket wrenches.

But we were determined to be fit enough to handle whatever challenge Denali presented. Not until we actually got to the mountain did we realize that running as much as we did was not the optimum preparation. You want to be a bulldog. I was basically a pencil neck.

Denali is reached via Anchorage and the little town of Talkeetna, where a plane takes you up to eight thousand feet, well above the tree line, to the Kahiltna Glacier, your starting point. Before they allow you to fly onto the mountain, you are required to attend a movie at ranger headquarters, highlighting the many perils ahead of you.

Dead bodies figure prominently in this film. It certainly reminds you that there is a potential downside to this particular form of recreation. In fact, there is one stretch on McKinley that for some time has proven particularly hazardous to Asian climbers. Many of them have fallen to their deaths there. It is known as the Orient Express. More mordant mountaineer humor.

When we got to Base Camp, Steve Young, our guide, took us to an enormous crevasse, where each of us was required to descend a line until we were hanging approximately thirty feet in free air. We then had to demonstrate we could climb back up the line and extract ourselves. Crevasses are a major fear and a constant danger on McKinley.

Our last act before pushing off was to bury the bottle of Wild Turkey that Ken brought with him, so that we'd have something appropriate with which to toast our triumphant return three weeks hence. I also had with me a water bottle filled with Jack Daniel's, which I blithely believed would make a nice accompaniment around our genteel campfires on the way up. I immediately discovered I was so trashed at the end of each day that I could hardly drool on myself, much less enjoy a glass of bourbon. About forty-eight hours into the climb I decided to rededicate the water bottle to its original purpose. I practically shed tears as I emptied the bourbon out into the snow.

The unvarying routine on the way up was to rope together, separated fifty to seventy feet, and then trudge along single file, an arrangement that minimizes the potential consequences of one member falling through the ice into a crevasse. Theoretically, the rest of the group provides sufficient traction to prevent more than one person from falling.

Everybody must move at the same pace to keep the line taut. In the good moments you just let your mind wander, and daydream. As you tire, however, all you think about is that frozen snake in front of you.

Our first major bivouac was the so-called Med Camp at 14,300 feet. Spread out across a shallow basin, Med Camp was a circus. Accessible in good weather by helicopter, it was teeming that first day with several teams of climbers, camera crews and even a few daredevils bold enough to try parasailing off the face. Ice sculptures and makeshift igloos dotted the scene.

Dominating all was the Ice Throne, a regal one-holer that

commands a glorious view of nearby Mount Foraker, generally regarded as the most magnificent prospect from any crapper in North America. I remember one night sitting on the Ice Throne as Foraker went into full, golden alpenglow before me. It was a moving experience.

The Ice Throne also undoubtedly is the highest-maintenance facility of its sort anywhere. It's raison d'être is removed by helicopter. (Everyone else must bag and deposit in crevasses.)

Because no tent can reliably withstand the arctic winds on McKinley, at each camp you must build a protective ice fort around you. But even a solid wall of ice blocks in time yields to the ceaseless blast, developing a serious case of the dwindles before crumbling altogether.

The day we arrived, we discovered the winds had swept an exhausted bird up to the Med Camp, where we found the disoriented animal perched shivering on a ski pole. We all knew our unbidden guest was a goner—there was no way it could get off the mountain before it starved or froze to death. Like that bird, we also were strangers in a strange land. It's impossible not to reflect on your own possible fate at such moments.

At dawn, we awoke to find three frozen bodies, roped together, lying out in the snow. It turned out they were British mountaineers who'd ignored several warnings the previous day that the weather conditions above Med Camp were too severe for climbing. They'd fallen to their deaths.

Again, it gave me pause to encounter three dead men halfway up my first serious mountain. But you have to understand the level of denial necessary to attempt McKinley in the first place. If I really accepted that I might get hurt, I wouldn't have gone.

Before we could try our luck on the slopes above us, we had business on the mountain below, a cache of food we'd left just below a place called Windy Corner, about a thousand vertical feet down McKinley from Med Camp. On our way to retrieve the cache, we passed a couple of guys who obviously had just come up. We gave them a big high five, waved and proceeded on our way.

Then the wind kicked up and soon was howling. Steve Young made it clear that we should take the storm seriously, and for the first time the thought really did cross my mind that we all could get killed like those Brits. It was very difficult to see or to move.

Anyway, we turned Windy Corner again on our way back up and there were the same two guys, just standing around like they were waiting for a bus. This time we walked over to them. I waved my hand right in front of their faces. No one home. This wasn't HACE. They were addlepated. As would later almost happen to me on the Balcony at Everest, they'd gotten very cold and just stopped. They couldn't make up their minds to go up or down. If we hadn't come along, they probably would have stood there until they froze to death.

One of the two was at least sentient enough to move his feet, so we tied him to the end of our climbing rope. Steve Young took a shorter piece of rope and tied it around the other one— who basically was not there at all—and pulled him up the mountain like a toy. When we all got back to Med Camp, we took them to the medical tent operated by Dr. Peter Hacket, a Colorado emergency room doctor who is also one of the world's premier experts on high-altitude physiology and a highly accomplished mountaineer.

From Med Camp we hauled our gear to the summit ridge, at approximately 16,400 feet, came back down and rested, then pushed up to High Camp, at 17,200 feet, where we built our ice walls and assembled ourselves and our equipment for the final push to the top.

Or so we thought.

The climb up had not been fun, and there was the added problem of the number-two guide, who had the distinct aura of an ex-con about him. I wouldn't have been surprised to see LOVE and HATE tattooed on his knuckles. We figured Steve had gotten the guy at a reduced rate. He grated on everyone's nerves.

But even that would have been sufferable had we actually accomplished what we'd gone through severe hardships to achieve. However, just as we were ready to go, high winds moved in, *very* high winds. The ambient temperature dropped to about forty below and stayed there, essentially trapping us in our sleeping bags.

Since the sun doesn't set on McKinley at that time of year, but sort of circles the mountain each day, our surroundings hardly varied as we tried to wait out the weather. The cold days passed slowly in the perpetual, monochromatic light, which shifted almost imperceptibly from light gray to dark gray and back again. I stirred from the bag's warmth only to relieve myself, discovering to my deep chagrin on each occasion that my hands would freeze before I could zip up. Every time I'd have to waddle back to the tent, climb in my bag and rewarm my hands until they were limber enough to pull up my zipper.

One morning, the wind died down for a bit. Ken and I excitedly started sorting our gear, thinking that finally we were headed up. Steve just looked at us, his hands in his pockets, and then spoke.

"There's going to be at least one stupid sonuvabitch who tries to climb this mountain today," he said. "But it sure as hell is not going to be me." Ken and I looked at each other and started unpacking. Sure enough, that wind came roaring back like a freight train.

As events on Mount Everest would later attest, one of the most important things a guide can tell you is when not to climb. Any fool can start up a hill. It takes real judgment and discipline to keep summit fever in check. Steve was not going to do something stupid.

We persevered at high camp until the food was gone, four long days, then started back down. The wind was blowing at about a hundred miles an hour. This was not going to be easy, especially with the bonehead complication I contrived to introduce.

Under very cold conditions, mountaineers not uncommonly pull on so-called vapor barrier socks—basically fancy trash-can liners—to keep their feet warm. Well, I had found an entire vapor barrier suit, which I had saved for the summit. When it was clear we were headed down, not up, in that frigid wind, I put on the suit—which made me resemble nothing so much as a human in a handy bag. But it certainly did keep me warm.

As we descended the fixed line that leads to high camp, I began to tire, rapidly. It was all I could do to stand up. I worried that I might fall. It took every bit of willpower to keep moving.

When we finally got to the bottom of the fixed line, Steve recognized that I was losing it. At one point, I did fall over, right on my keister.

"Give me your pack," he said, and I did. He put a loop around it and walked off, dragging my pack through the snow. This was a thoroughly shameful episode. Everyone but me was pulling his load. I would walk back to camp looking like a complete fool. I was mortified, and fell two or three more times before we got down to Med Camp.

There, Steve took me to Dr. Hacket. Inside, I unzipped my suit to discover I was completely drenched in sweat, chin to toes. I'd created a portable steam cabinet, cooking myself like a Chinese dumpling.

"Why in the world are you wearing that thing?" asked Hacket, who measured my resting pulse at 160.

A couple of glasses of tea revived me somewhat, followed by some soup and a lot more tea, more than two liters of it.

The strangest part of the experience was that though I was obviously very dehydrated, I hadn't once been thirsty, just weakened. I don't understand the physiology of it.

We started walking again, with the wind howling louder and louder. About a thousand feet below Windy Corner we at last made camp, for which I was deeply grateful. I didn't feel real good. When I pulled off my boots, I discovered they were sloshing in sweat. I was like those fishermen in the cartoons who pour fish out of their boots. As I got into my bag, I smelled myself for the first time, an overpowering odor of ammonia. I'd been burning muscle like crazy.

Next morning, the storm was still blowing heavy. Our idea was to get beneath it. So we put on snowshoes and started down again.

McKinley was the first mountain where my glasses were a

problem. After they fogged up and froze over a couple of times, I didn't wear them at all, which meant that I saw very little. The guys later kidded me that I could have gone downtown and gotten in a freezer and sat there for three weeks for all I was able to see on McKinley. That was largely true.

Now it was blowing so hard that I repeatedly got this mask of ice across my face. I had to put my thumbs into my eye sockets to pop open my lids or my eyes would freeze shut. For some stupid reason, I didn't think to wear goggles.

Pretty soon I was operating on automatic, just putting one foot in front of the other. I was so exhausted and concentrating so hard that my world shrank to a radius of two or three feet. At one point we passed a dog team on the trail and I didn't even notice. Not long thereafter I walked out of one of my snowshoes and immediately sank up to my chest. Steve was furious with me, and gave me a pretty fair tongue-lashing as we dug the snowshoe out of five feet of snow.

We marched on through the blizzard, all of us sensing our gathering peril. Steve finally stopped and said, bluntly, "We have a big problem. I have no idea if we are still on the right trail. We're going to have to dig in."

The wind was blowing way too strong for us to erect tents. So we spent the next ten hours digging a hole down into the glacier. We excavated on our hands and knees to a depth of about ten feet, then hollowed out a snow cave large enough to accommodate all six of us. It was brutal work.

When we finally got into our sleeping bags and warmed up a little, I began feeling the pain of someone repeatedly slamming a ball peen hammer into my fingertips. I'd frozen them while digging but hadn't noticed. Now my newly thawed nerve endings were emphatically informing me of the damage they'd suffered. As it turned out, several of my fingers were frostbitten down to the cuticle.

Cecilia Boone:

Ken later told us of a conversation he had with Beck in that snow cave.

"Okay," he said, "we need to decide right now whether we're ever doing any of this again. I'm thinking we shouldn't. This is hell. This is miserable. This is not worth it."

Beck said, "No, you can't make that decision now. You have to wait until the end, when you're back home. This is not the time."

Ken said, "Hell, *yes,* it is!"

We slept about six hours and then dug out of our cave. The storm had finally let up. The rest of the walk down to Base Camp was uneventful, save for the last little part, called Heartbreak Hill. Incoming aircraft meet the Kahiltna Glacier on a downward slope, meaning that the last mile of your return from the mountain actually is uphill, an unwelcome final test of your endurance.

It turned out that another group was coming down the same time as we were. Steve's ex-con second-in-command suddenly decided to pick up our pace in order to beat these other guys to the finish. This was high-school-Harry stuff. At this point, with each step I was mumbling over and over to myself a parody from *The Wizard of Oz;* to wit, "Hamburgers, steaks, french fries, oh my!" But Ken and Ed Clark, one of our fellow climbers, were steamed. They started yelling unpleasant things at the guide.

When we finally got to camp, Ed and Ken nearly came to blows over which one would get to beat the living stuffing out of the ex-con. Eventually, they both simmered down, a process mightily abetted by the superchilled Wild Turkey that Ken liberated from the snowbank. Imagine what kind of buzz two guys in our shape can get from straight bourbon at eight thousand feet. Eventually we invited the other two guys over and they helped us finish it off.

As we discussed the expedition, their general view was that they never wanted to see a place like that again. Ken and I kept saying, "Wow! Wasn't that great!"

We thought it was just wonderful.

Ken Zornes:

We even laughed about that conversation in the ice cave. After we got home and healed, we forgot all about that.

Nineteen

When we got back to Dallas, everyone met us at the airport with champagne. Then we went out to dinner. Peach wasn't as interested in celebrating as some of the others. I'm not sure she realized that I was going to continue doing this.

Peach:

He was exhilarated—beat all to hell, frostbitten and exhilarated. I thought a little pain was a good thing. I didn't realize what was happening. Later, Beck told some McKinley war stories at a party. Mike Mack, one of the thoracic surgeons at the hospital, said it sounded to him like Beck had had an attack of pulmonary edema.

Beck doesn't talk much about his infirmities. He said that he had only been a little dehydrated. Mack said that wasn't true.

I had a few rales, lung noises. I never thought I had edema.

Terry White:

It was after McKinley that we started worrying about the mountain climbing. He sat up there for four days, almost getting blown off the mountain. Got some frostbite. When that didn't slow him down at all and he started planning his next climb, I wondered about his reasoning, whether he was thinking about his family.

It's one thing to risk your life. Some people are driven to do it. In those circumstances, would I? Certainly not. This bothered us.

Mountain climbing didn't replace ocean sailing as my passion so much as it temporarily displaced it, or postponed it—at least in my strategic thinking.

I saw the need to prioritize these things in a temporal sense. I could sail when I was sixty, but I wouldn't be climbing mountains. I was in my early forties, and I very much realized that I had a decade at most when I could reasonably expect my body to work. If I wanted to explore any of that stuff, now was the time to do it.

So I dropped the sailing back fifteen or twenty years. All the time I was climbing I still maintained the same sailing training: I continued to read avidly.

In the winter of 1990 I headed south to climb two volcanoes in Mexico, both conveniently located a cab ride away from Mexico City. Popocatepl (17,887 feet) and neighboring Pico de Orizaba (18,700 feet) are not tough climbs, although you should have glacier experience before attempting them. They are generally considered good warm-ups for more challenging peaks, such as Denali, so I expected a comparatively simple time of it in Mexico.

But I learned it is unwise to take a big mountain for granted. "El Popo," for example, suddenly began erupting four years after I climbed it, and is now indefinitely closed to mountaineers. Five climbers who came to film the eruptions died on the mountain in May of 1996.

The more subtle lesson that I took away from Popocatepl was how everything needs to click in order for you to get to the top; how fragile and contingent you are on a climb; how easily things can go awry; how something that would be a minor annoyance at sea level can be dramatically amplified at high altitude. Take, for instance, the common stomach bug—please.

We did the usual altitude acclimatization program on Popocatepl, and settled into the hut from which we'd launch our summit assault. That evening, a dozen or so mice began running around inside my belly. I'm experienced with the feeling, and recognized what was ahead long before I got to enjoy the full moment.

They hit me in the middle of the night. I headed for the bathroom, selected a stall and stayed there serenading the commode until dawn. I was careful to lock the stall door. There was no way they were going to get me out of there alive.

Another guy was in there with me, too, making animal noises. It was dawn before the vomiting subsided enough for me to crawl back into my bunk.

I spent the day praying for relief. The idea of food set me retching. But as our appointed departure hour approached, the other guy, a kid in his twenties, pulled on his boots and prepared to climb. This was not something I had considered possible. But I'd be damned if I'd let this kid leave me sitting there.

So I rolled out of bed, assuming I'd make it about a quarter mile before I barfed again and then would have a manly excuse for diving back into the rack. To my surprise, however, I did not buckle as expected. The kid and a couple of other guys started retching on the trail—the bug was going around—and quit the climb. I soldiered on with the rest of the group. It took forever, but finally we made it to the top.

It was late in the day by then, so part of the way down we were in pitch darkness. Feeling better as we went along, I joined one of the guides in a trot to the hut, where we rejoiced at the discovery that someone had turned on the hot water.

After El Popo we climbed Pico de Orizaba without incident, and I headed back home for Texas more certain than ever that I'd found my métier in mountaineering. The sport fulfilled me on several levels. I loved its simplicity and how it took me completely outside the boundaries of my day-to-day existence. It remained my refuge from the dull ache of depression, which still isolated me back in Dallas, but was becoming more manageable now that I knew how to pry myself loose from it from time to time.

It was also a delight to discover that my combination of physical and mental toughness could carry me where some younger, stronger and more physically talented climbers weren't able to go. I didn't measure myself against them. As I said, mountaineering is not a competitive sport.

I didn't feel superior, either. I was pleased to be welcome in their company, and to acquit myself well when challenges arose. It was a tremendous ego boost for someone who'd spent so much time focused on his limitations to go where only a select handful of very tough and determined athletes had been.

There was also the sheer thrill of facing down my demons.

I usually didn't get scared in the mountains unless I was belayed. I remember one time dangling from these little gadgets crammed into the rock face, about three hundred feet up, with birds flying below me.

Have I *entirely* lost my mind? I wondered.

On a Colorado climb with Ken Zornes and Steve Young, we were on a pretty steep face when lightning, high wind and freezing rain suddenly came up. We were wearing T-shirts and shorts, standing on a perhaps half-inch-wide crack.

Steve decided it was too dangerous to continue on up, so a rappel down an unfamiliar face was going to be our exit route. The belay was a thumblet of rock, over which Young put a quarter inch of webbing, attached himself and rappelled away. Ken was next, leaving me alone up there in that storm, hugging the rock and wondering how my obituary was going to look. I comforted myself that there are worse ways to check out. It was better than being run down while riding a moped.

This may have been the single most terrifying moment in my life, confronting my ultimate fear. I pushed off—making sure not to push *too* far lest the webbing pull free of the thumblet— and quickly descended to where Steve and Ken were hanging in free space, bolted to the side of the hill.

I didn't let on how terrified I was, and managed to control a bad case of the shakes until later, when no one was watching. I now understand that I wanted that terror. At the time I would have denied it. It was a jolt, no question. You can really get juiced by something that frightening.

Peach:

In the spring of 1991, Beck and I and the children flew to Boston to revisit our first home. Beck had a meeting to attend as well. Afterward, we put Meg and Beck on the plane for Dallas, and then went back to our hotel. Beck said he needed to talk to me.

"I'm suicidal," he disclosed. "And the problem is our marriage. I'm real unhappy and it is your fault."

At this stage of our relationship, I was still willing to believe that. There wasn't a night for five years that I had not cried about it, but I didn't blame him. I was sure I was at fault for whatever was wrong. I asked him if he'd explain it to me.

"You're not supportive of me," he said. "You're not supportive of my hobbies. I think you love me, but I don't think you like me."

That last sentence gave me pause. I wondered if it might be true.

I did tell her I was so damned depressed that I thought I was going to do myself in. But I don't think I dumped my depression on her so much as I laid it open to her, revealed what was very, very difficult for me to reveal.

I didn't see her problems with me as any kind of failure on her part. And I don't recall ever feeling that the cause of my depression was our relationship. However, I wouldn't be the least bit surprised if that is what she took away from that conversation.

I'd been hiding the fact I was miserable for a long time. But it was not my intention to say, "What's wrong with us is you." Or, "What's wrong with me is you."

Peach:

I think he was looking for a way to ditch all of us.

That's not true!

Peach:

You said you were depressed, and that it was my fault.

I was suicidal. Peach told me that I needed help. Even though this was the last thing I would do on my own, I made an effort. I knew the wife of a colleague at the hospital was a psychiatrist, and I thought I could get some idea from her of who to talk to. She gave me a guy's name.

Peach:

This psychologist was terrified. Beck told him he was suicidal, and that two members of his family, a cousin and a great-uncle, had committed suicide, although he tried to justify it.

I wasn't trying to justify anything. My cousin was a juvenile diabetic. I think my great-uncle was concerned about becoming a burden to somebody. He didn't think he was going to be able to take care of himself. So he gave his gun to my father to clean, then took it back and shot himself. I did tell this psychologist that I always thought I'd die by my own hand.

Peach:

Beck came back from seeing him and told me I had to go see him, too, because everything wrong was related to our marriage. So I went, and the guy seemed absolutely sure that Beck was going to kill himself. He said we had to get rid of all the guns in the house.

There was a shotgun, a .22 rifle, a .38 revolver, a .357 Magnum, a .22 pistol, a little Derringer and a pellet gun. They all went to the police, including the pellet gun, which I'd never quite thought of in that context.

Peach:

Still, I feared for Beck, not so much because he was suicidal—that obviously was a concern—but because he couldn't feel our love. I felt enormous sadness that he didn't like himself, and felt he had to prove himself. He couldn't just go out and enjoy the sunrise and sunset. He couldn't enjoy the little things. Beck could only proceed from goal to goal. That makes for a very unhappy person.

Twenty

The order in which I chose the mountains to climb belies my claim of careful thought and planning. Denali was spontaneous folly. If I had been going about this business in a logical way, El Popo and Pico de Orizaba would have preceded it. In truth, my choices were dictated for the most part by the availability of a competently led expedition to a suitable peak at a convenient date. These factors in combination brought me in August of 1991 to Mount Elbrus in the Caucasus Mountains.

These were the dying days of the Evil Empire, and Moscow even in summertime was a cold, gray, dismal place. Bizarre, too. For instance, strict foreign-exchange restrictions complicated the simplest purchases. On a visit to Moscow's Olympic Stadium I encountered a man selling lacquered boxes displayed on a blanket. After the usual haggling to set a price, he gave me my box and an empty cigarette pack and instructed me to walk around for a while before placing the agreed-upon amount of U.S. currency in the pack, which I was then to discard in some nearby bushes for him to retrieve.

The leader of our climbing group was an unusual character named Sergio Fitz Watkins, who claimed to be part Mexican, part Apache and part something else. Sergio was a handful. For some reason, he didn't want to have his picture taken, nor was he into collegial relationships. Sergio let you know that he was the boss and you weren't, and would go to extremes to dramatize his issues.

Sergio commonly began climbing days with the statement, "Today is a good day to die."

People keep stealing my lines.

From Moscow we flew to the republic of Kabardino-Balkar, and were bused to a ski resort near the base of Mount Elbrus. At 18,481 feet, it is the tallest mountain in Europe. That's the only reason I was there.

I remember along the way we made a pit stop at a shack that served as a comfort station, even though inside there was nothing but a dirt floor.

The hotel food was dreadful. One day for lunch we were served a pile of formless, colorless vegetables of some sort. Then I was given a slab of meat, except that it was not meat. It was a half-inch-thick, four-inch-wide slice of fat.

Our first night, I looked out my third-floor balcony to see a little kid standing on a four- or five-inch ledge, offering to sell me ice screws made of titanium from the nearby titanium mine, the largest in the world.

Then we all went looking for something to drink. In a country famous for its alcoholics, you'd think that would be a simple task.

Uh-uh.

There was no vodka or other strong drink available at our hotel, so we lit out with our packs to the *piva* store. *Piva* is Russian for "beer." They give *piva* away on their airlines for one good reason: No one with a choice would ever pay for it.

They also have a thing they call wine, but it is easily mistaken for something a domestic animal with kidney problems might produce. So we loaded up at the *piva* store and came clanking back with our Russian beer.

The climb began with a ski-lift ride about a mile up the mountain to a round, metal-skinned hut that resembled an immense circular airstream trailer. Called Priut (Russian for "refuge"), the structure was built in 1939, just in time for the German army to shoot up the place on its marches to and from the Soviet oil fields on the Caspian Sea.

When we encountered Priut, the place was a pigsty. Water, if you dared drink it, had to be retrieved from the middle of a melt pool outside the front door. The latrine, ankle-deep in feces, lay just beyond. It was an act of grace when Priut was later destroyed in a gas fire.

We did one acclimatization hike, then arose the next night for the assault, which is a long slog up a snow trail. It was very cold. When we came to a saddle at about sixteen thousand feet, a young lawyer from Dallas looked like he was getting ready to lose consciousness. Another member of our group, a plastic surgeon from Atlanta, had a hell of a headache. So he and the lawyer headed back together, a perfectly fine plan except the kid then proceeded to take a big old dumper in his suit on the way down.

This was not at all what the brochure promised.

As the rest of us pushed on to the summit, I thought of a photo in my fellow Dallasite Dick Bass's mountain-climbing memoir, *The Seven Summits*. It is a bronze head of Lenin, mounted on a wonderful pedestal at the very top of Elbrus. Eager to behold this memorial for myself, when we finally summitted I was instead reminded that this was, after all, the Soviet Union. The pedestal still stood, but Lenin's likeness was long gone, a pipe wrench left in its place.

The customary post-climb celebration was held in Moscow in a huge room that looked like the hall of mirrors at Versailles. There was a big table right in the center, sumptuously laden with food, Russian champagne, pitchers of vodka, white and black caviar. It was an incredible meal.

There were other little tables all around the room. I assumed they were for other patrons, later. Sure enough, people did start coming in, most of them pairs of young women, who sat down and ordered aperitifs.

I thought, How nice! Muscovites out on the town! Then I realized that *all* of the tables had two young women each. Our big table began to disperse as various guys went to sit down with these gals. Slow as I am, I finally did figure out there was a second course to that meal—intercourse. They were all working girls.

No way was Spotless McFarland here going to hook up with one of these war brides, only to be taken aside and rubber-truncheoned by the KGB. But evidently such fears did not dissuade every member of our group. When I got back to our hotel, my roommate was missing in action.

Peach:

Family vacations pretty much stopped when he started climbing. There were occasional days at the beach. We went to Cancun once, and he had to leave early. That changed the dynamic of the trip. When he left, everyone else was flat and unhappy. We ended up coming home a day early.

After a while, my brother Howie, together with his wife, Pat, and daughter, Laura, would join the children and me on vacations. He wasn't there to replace Beck. But it was wonderful to have Howie around to talk to. Also, he was always a treat for the kids. He'd dream up things to do for them, keep them entertained all day. This was something that Beck never did. Howie made a big difference in their lives, and mine, too.

Meg:

Uncle Howie always came through Dallas on business trips, and he'd fix everything that was broken in our house. He fixed the basketball backboard, my dad's shower and put in an underground drainage system for us.

He refused to see the bad side of me, and was supportive of everything I did. I mean, he and his wife, Pat, came all the way from Georgia to see me in my eighth-grade musical. He'd play dominoes with me—which I never really understood—and he brought me Pixy Stix, little colored tubes of, like, pure sugar.

Bub:

Uncle Howie was the kind of guy who'd take my sister and me off our parents' hands after dinner so they could relax and enjoy themselves without having to worry about entertaining us.

When he came to town and went to work fixing things, he and I sometimes would go to the store to pick up any necessary parts and material. One particular time—I was about nine or ten—we needed to go to Target to find some automotive parts; Howie was going to repair one of our cars.

He didn't know the directions to Target, but I thought I did and said so, even though my knowledge of Dallas at that time was a bit vague. I quickly got us lost.

We'd head one direction for a while, until it was clear to me we'd gone too far, then we'd U-turn and head back. Most people would have let me continue like this a time or two before pulling over to call my mom for help.

Howie didn't. He patiently allowed me to figure it out for myself. Every time we had to make a U-turn, he'd make a joke and then drive in whatever direction I said. Eventually, we did make it to Target, and it meant the world to me that Howie believed enough in my ability to get us there.

Peach:

I doubt that Beck even realized we were taking vacations without him, much less that Howie and his family were now coming along, too. Beck was totally wrapped up in himself. I remember one time when I was feeling desperate, there was an $88 round-trip super-cheap flight to New Orleans. Our friends the Ketchersids were going to go with us, except Beck couldn't possibly leave work early Friday afternoon to catch the flight.

Then we discovered he had the week off and didn't even know it. I was furious with him.

The only thing he was aware of was his climbing. He became very odd. His attitude was "You don't bother me with anything. Kids. Problems. Anything."

In January of 1992, I headed south again, this time to Aconcagua in the Argentine Andes. At 22,831 feet, Aconcagua is the tallest mountain in the Western Hemisphere, and the sixty-third tallest peak in the world. All the taller hills are in Asia.

The novelist Trevanian maligns Aconcagua in his thriller *The Eiger Sanction* as "a vast heap of rotten rock and ice. It destroys men, not with the noble counterstrokes of an Eigerwand or a Nanga Partbat, but by eroding a man's nerve and body until he is a staggering, whimpering maniac."

Trevanian's right. Aconcagua is a nasty place. I can't imagine anyone wanting to climb it more than once.

I signed on with Mountain Travel-Sobeck, the same California outfit that had organized the Elbrus climb, and was thus reunited with the prickly Señor Watkins, who on this occasion was considerably less demonstrative, possibly because he had contracted a nasty virus. He wouldn't make it to the top.

You fly first to Buenos Aires. From there, the next stop is the mountain city of Mendoza, which proved a culture shock for me. Training for the climb, I'd been rising at 4:00 A.M. and going to bed at 7:30 P.M. You couldn't buy *lunch* at 7:30 P.M. in

Mendoza. I saw people out walking around with their families until two and three in the morning.

We drove in a pickup to a partially completed ski resort, where our gear was loaded onto mules for the twenty-mile trek to Aconcagua Base Camp. As we headed out on foot, we passed the climbers' cemetery. They were packed in there pretty tight.

At the end of the scruffy dirt trail was Plaza de Mulas, sort of the local Lobuje equivalent. Instead of yaks you got mules, and mule dung was everywhere. Unlike Lobuje, there were no permanent structures at Plaza de Mulas. We encountered a hundred or so people of widely varying experience and seriousness—I saw one woman dressed in a pink snowsuit carrying her little poodle—all formed into a haphazard tent village.

There was a small watering hole, similar to what they call a tank in Texas, which seemed to serve a variety of communal uses, from drinking to washing to excretion. You got the impression that no one was particularly concerned about disease. You also wanted to be very careful not to face the wind with your mouth open. There was so much toilet paper floating around in the air—Aconcagua snowbirds—that you risked sucking up a wad of it.

Plaza de Mulas was sickness waiting to erupt, and we did not want to linger in that swamp a moment longer than necessary. As it was, one member of our group developed the pestilential hellhole trots and had to be removed by emergency helicopter.

My most dramatic recollection of the place had nothing to do with filth and disease, however. We were standing around one day when suddenly there came a deep rumble in the distance. I looked up to see a huge waterfall where there had been nothing two seconds before. An enormous river was thundering down the face of the mountain. You could see the waves rolling along, glistening in the sun.

Then as I looked at it more closely, I realized the torrent wasn't water at all, but rock! This whole mass flowing just like whitewater rapids actually *was* rock, a *huge* rock slide flowing along a couple hundred feet from us.

We didn't get very far up Aconcagua before Sergio let us know he was too sick to continue. Halfway to the top, we came to a flat open area and a little hut, where we encountered a group of climbers on their way down. As it happened, they, too, were a Mountain-Sobeck group, led by Ricardo Novallo Torrez, a guide distinguished for being the first Mexican to summit Everest.

Sergio announced that he was packing it in at this point, leaving our group in the questionable care of his second-in-command, a Peruvian named Augusto Ortega, who didn't speak much English. Torrez, although he'd already climbed Aconcagua and was whupped, saw that the job of taking us up was probably too much for Ortega. He volunteered to accompany the group as far as High Camp, whence the Peruvian would shepherd us the rest of the way to the summit and back.

When the wind picked up and the ambient temperature plummeted, some of the less experienced among us reasonably began to worry about frostbite and their general inability to keep warm. I lacked their commonsense approach to this deepening discomfort. Having been pinned to the top of Denali when it was unhappy, I knew there was a whole other level of cold beyond this point that was well within my comfort range.

No surprise, then, that when we started out for the summit together, we were a herd of turtles. Soon realizing that the eight of us would never make it to the top at that speed, the group retreated into High Camp for a parley. Half the climbers wanted to quit. I and three other guys wanted to try again. So that is what we did.

One of those who headed back down the mountain was my tent mate, an old guy who absentmindedly took with him my single eating utensil, a spoon. Since the dog-food gruel we consumed on the mountain required an instrument for shoveling it into your mouth, I went outside in search of a suitable replacement.

Nosing around, I spied a metal handle sticking out of the snow. I grabbed it, braced myself, shouted, "Excaliber!" and gave a good yank. Out popped a fork, missing a tine or two, but perfectly usable. I wiped it under my armpit and returned to the tent, once again a functioning member of the final four.

Well after dark that night, probably around ten o'clock, an improbable visitor showed up. He was Marty Schmidt, a New Zealander, who'd just guided two policemen up and down the mountain.

"Hey! Anybody there?" Marty shouted. He was in his climbing gear and sneakers. "Can I borrow some boots?" Marty also had a bicycle over his shoulder.

We loaned him the boots and off he went. About five or six the next morning, Marty came back, without the bicycle. He returned the boots, put his sneakers back on and walked back to Plaza de Mulas to rejoin his two clients.

As we later learned, the story of Marty's remarkable double climb of Aconcagua—he hadn't slept in two days—actually began at a hellacious stretch called the Caneletta, a huge, forty-five-degree hill of dirt and loose rock just below the summit.

Schmidt and the policemen had discovered a bicycle strewn in pieces all over the Caneletta: a wheel here, pedals there, handlebars somewhere else. I don't know if Marty pondered the mystery behind this unlikely discovery. But being a practical person, he gathered all the parts, assembled them, put the machine on his back and carried it down with him.

Now here's the surprise. When he got to Plaza de Mulas with the bike, a complete stranger accosted him, angrily, accusing him of stealing his bicycle!

"What do you mean, stealing your bicycle?" Marty asked. "There were parts lying all over the mountain."

It turned out that this guy had been paying people to carry the bike up Aconcagua, one piece at a time. Once all the parts were up there, he intended to assemble the vehicle and then ride it down from the summit. He might even have had a sponsorship. Who knows?

Nonplussed, Marty proposed a solution.

"Okay, I'll make you a deal," he told the guy. "Stop screaming at me for stealing your bicycle and I will take it back to where I got it."

That's what he did that night. Schmidt carried the bike all the way back nearly to the summit, disassembled it in the dark, strewed the pieces around, and then climbed down again. It was, among other things, a physical tour de force. Marty Schmidt is a very strong climber.

Next day, weather conditions had not improved, but now only four of us and Augusto were heading up the trail. At no point had this been a pretty or even interesting climb, but when we finally reached the Caneletta, I understood why Trevanian so fiercely loathes Aconcagua.

The Caneletta may be the most miserable natural incline on earth. You can't go up it quickly, because you can't get enough breath. But if you go too slowly, it slides out from under you.

The trick is to move from rock to rock, looking for one with some traction. When you hit a magic stone that doesn't move, you stand there gasping for air long enough to get your heart out of your throat and back into your chest. Then you move on, often losing three steps for every one you gain, and you do this for a number of hours. It is not fun.

Three days were needed to climb from Plaza de Mulas to High Camp, plus an added overnight for our second assault, and then another day to get back down. I had been training very hard, however, and could feel the cumulative effect of all that work.

I felt really good after summiting Aconcagua. I was ahead of the pack on the way down, and got to a place where a finger of rock sits on the traverse that heads across to the Caneletta. I stopped for some water and M&M's.

An Australian in our group came along behind me and fell over on his back, as if he were dead. Finally, he rose on an elbow and said to me, "Are you in as good a shape as you seem to be? Or are you just taking better drugs than the rest of us?"

Peach:

We probably wouldn't have stay married but for the kids. Children really need two parents. They need balance in their lives. They need fathers to roll around on the floor and horse around with them. Learning how to play is important. Both of my kids are fairly cautious. They didn't have anybody to tell them to take risks, take chances, be physical.

You also have to understand that no one in my family has ever been divorced. No one. The word was not in my vocabulary. I thought of divorce as a failure—a major one.

I remember my mother telling me stories about old Miz So-and-So. Her husband used to run around on her but she stuck with him, she said, and now he's sick and they're together. It's nice to be old and have somebody.

Something else occurred to me then. You *ought* to know that you have to work on a marriage. One of my friends, Victoria Bryhan, is locally famous for a remark she made while we were discussing somebody who was getting a divorce.

"Why is she getting divorced?" Victoria asked. "She'll just marry another man."

That is the truth.

My friends became a great source of strength to me. Victoria and Pat White and Linda Gravelle. Mary Ann Bristow (who also has family in Georgia), Marianne Ketchersid and Cecilia Boone. There were lots of them, mostly mothers of children who went to school with my children. We saw a lot of each other. Somehow, this sisterhood emerged, which is interesting since I had no sisters as a child, and didn't even join a sorority in college.

I could be very frank with them. Most people don't want to tell you what's really going on in their lives. Looking around, it is easy to think that everyone is okay *but* you. That's just not true. If you really sit down in a soul-baring discussion, everyone has her little story to tell. And I think the stories can be shared without male-bashing and -slamming. I suspect the same thing is true for men.

I could not, however, confide in anyone else, particularly my family. Even Howie would not have understood. This was a challenge I'd face with a lot of help from my friends.

Our discussions would start with, "*I* would *never* let my husband do that!" I'd say, "Well, tell me how to stop it! I'm open." Pretty soon it became "My husband doesn't do *that,* but let me tell you what he *does* do."

I built emotional bridges to these women, my buddies, because I needed to talk. I needed to express my confusion and my anger. And in the process, I discovered that *everybody* has problems. You realize everyone has a different twist; we're all plodding along the same road with slightly different stories. *Father Knows Best* doesn't exist and, for us, neither does Prince Charming.

Another woman I knew was going through a divorce. Someone else had a total breakdown; I was really surprised because I would have thought this woman was one of the strong ones. Still another had a control-freak husband. We saw one's husband in a restaurant with another woman. Another's husband was having a long-term affair; I'd thought she had the strongest marriage of any of us. One was having a ton of problems with a younger brother whom she and her husband had to support.

Another one, who really wasn't a friend, revealed her husband was an alcoholic and had to have an intervention.

The perfect marriage probably doesn't exist. As with kids, you've got to work at it, even if working at it seems to get you nowhere, the way it got me nowhere. I still preach that, because I don't want people giving up too soon.

Our after-Aconcagua dinner and party was held in Mendoza. We went to a nice place just a few blocks from our hotel, and drank a whole lot of *cervezas*. One of the guys had a jug of Jack Daniel's and we passed that around.

Dinner was over by eleven or twelve. The sane members of our group headed for the hotel. The three or four who remained, including myself, voted one more for the mountain. I was already more than moderately buzzed.

One of the guys, my roommate, drank a layered parfait thing and started baying at the moon. We'd invaded a quiet, family bar, as I recall, and there he was, holding on to the rail with both hands, baying at the moon. I thought maybe it was time for me to leave.

Besides being inebriated, I was night blind. Within five minutes I also was lost. An hour and a half later I wandered into a bus station I recognized as our point of departure from Mendoza to the mountain several days before. I had the sense to get a taxi cab for the brief ride to the hotel and my room, where I discovered that my parfait-quaffing roomie had vomited everywhere.

So much for the romance of the high country.

For me our boozy revel around Mendoza was not the trip's true exclamation point. That had occurred the night before at the ski lodge. After we walked out the twenty miles from Plaza de Mulas, we enjoyed a good dinner at the lodge and drank some mescal that could take the enamel off your teeth.

We all then got in the sauna and sat there swapping mountain stories. At one point, I turned to Ricardo and asked him what it takes to try Everest. He casually answered, "Well, somebody like you could do it."

A little light went on. This was a watershed moment.

So far my interest in mountain climbing hardly had been dilettantish; I had worked very hard and prepared well for each climb. But now, uncharacteristically big dreams started crowding into my consciousness. Depending upon your perspective, this was the beginning, or the beginning of the end, for me.

My thoughts quickly focused on two connected objectives. I decided that I would point my training and my climbing toward the ultimate goal—Everest—and in the process attempt what Dick Bass and very few others had so far accomplished, the Seven Summits Quest. Bass had accomplished the Seven Summits in four years. With a huge dose of luck, I thought, the inconceivable might become reality and I would join that elite circle.

Such grand plans were highly unusual for one so cautious. I can account for the departure on a number of levels. First, my depression was by now fading. It hadn't vanished altogether—I still felt dreadful most of the time I was home—but it was not nearly the same crushing presence it had been, and I believed the mountains were responsible for that. Although my response to the depression surely added to my family's pain and my estrangement from them, it could reasonably be argued that mountaineering saved my life.

I also had discovered how much I enjoyed the company of high-altitude mountaineers. They have traits in common that I admire. For example, this kind of climbing entails misery. There's not a lot of bitching and carrying on. They also tend to be fairly driven, and usually they're successful at whatever their life's work might be.

It takes a lot of effort and mental maturity to climb a big hill. It is not something you do on natural gifts alone. You've got to learn the skills. High-altitude climbers must enjoy putting themselves in situations where they're not sure how they're going to respond. It is one of the most intriguing aspects of this type of climbing. No matter how good you are, you're never sure you can do it. You're testing yourself. You hope you will be honorable, that you won't fall apart, that you'll maintain, that your courage won't desert you, that you'll give fully of what you have. But you don't know until the moment of truth. At some level you fear that when tested you'll prove a person of little character, nothing but a coward.

Third, I had handled Aconcagua with ease. This was a big mountain, and every time it challenged me—as on the Caneletta—I had plenty with which to respond. I felt strong. Moreover, I had gone to nearly 23,000 feet without experiencing a single problem with altitude. Objectively, I could agree with Torrez that I seemed to have enough of the right stuff to try Everest.

Fourth, not unlike most males, I needed to measure myself against something concrete and external, like a mountain. Earlier in my life, I'd collected degrees and certificates, and accumulated numerous high-gloss artifacts of the good life. Now I had bolder, and grander, aspirations.

Had I been emotionally whole I would have recognized that last sentence was nonsense. There was stark incompatibility between my risky pleasure seeking and my responsibilities as a husband and father of children. Rationally, that is not a difficult concept to grasp. But if you are blind to the natural imperatives of fatherhood, if like me you cannot see how your family vitally requires you, then it's a relatively simple thing to desert them. After that ego stroke from Torrez, if I *genuinely* had a better opinion of myself, there would have been no need to climb any more mountains.

Instead, I was not to be deterred.

I had been training approximately eighteen hours a week, not really understanding much about the business of getting into top shape. As a result, I probably had done myself as much harm as good. Both my shoulders ached all the time, and I could not sleep on my left side. One knee was gimpy as hell from arthritis. I could barely run five miles on it.

I gradually decided I was incapable of real strength. I didn't know if it was my muscle fiber or my frame or whatever, but I worked harder than anyone ever seen in that gym and yet I rapidly plateaued at a pretty pitiful level of strength. The max

I could bench-press was maybe 210. Small girls bench-press that kind of weight. I have real tiny bones.

Furthermore, I now faced an unusual problem of bulk that I was unsure how to address. I knew from my conversations and reading that most climbers lose about thirty pounds on Everest. Since I weighed about 150 pounds at the time, I was clearly too slight. Somehow, I needed to increase my weight by one fifth, and those extra pounds had to be all muscle or I didn't stand a chance on Everest. Plus I wanted endurance. On a mountain, you want to be able to destroy your muscles and then use them the next day.

Oddly enough, it was Peach who found my solution for me.

Peach:

In 1990, I was diagnosed with osteoporosis. Part of my doctor's program for me to add bone mass was weight training, which I began with the help of Brent Blackmore, a personal trainer. Within two years, I had completely restored my bone density. Brent is a very careful and accomplished trainer.

Over that same period, I watched as Beck gradually destroyed his body. He was working out eighteen hours a week and going lame in the process. He believed that no pain equalled no gain, which added up to no brain.

I recommended that he try a trainer. Beck said personal trainers were for sissies, or something to that effect. But I kept after him until one day he reluctantly agreed to go see Brent.

Brent Blackmore:

Beck couldn't understand why Peach had to have a personal trainer. She finally told him, "Well, I'm not the one who's injured, am I?" Beck already had messed up both his rotator cuffs, probably by trying to lift too much, with poor technique. He was recklessly trying to get stronger.

Peach said to me, "Would you be willing to work with my husband, Beck?"

I'd never met him. She set up the appointment for 9:00 A.M. on a Saturday, and he reluctantly came to see me.

He said he was training for Everest. I'd never trained a mountain climber before, nor had I ever worked with an adult athlete getting ready to take on something so big. It was a big challenge.

After the first workout, he left without saying a word.

Frankly, I thought personal trainers were for bored housewives. Brent and I sort of eyed each other. He was obviously fit, practiced what he preached, but I still didn't really believe I needed this stuff. When he was done with me that first day, I was just about able to get to the car before I threw up.

Brent Blackmore:

In the middle of the next week, Peach asked me if I had time to work with Beck again.

He came in, worked out, walked out and didn't say anything.

Peach had set up a third appointment for him. Finally, he asked me himself if I could train him.

Beck wasn't in very good shape. If I recall, at the time he had to sleep on his left side because his right shoulder hurt so much. He had to put a pillow between his side and his right elbow. If he rolled out of that position, he'd wake up in pain. His right knee bothered him, too. There were certain exercises we had to avoid at the start.

After a while, Beck said, "You know, it's a long way from Saturday to Saturday. Can you work with me during the week?" So we started doing 5:30 A.M. workouts on Tuesdays and Thursdays.

I really beat him up, and I showed him he could do more in three hours a week than he had been doing in eighteen. He discovered that he was so sore on Wednesday mornings after working with me on Tuesdays that he couldn't get out of bed to go work out, as he usually did. Beck was also afraid of working out Wednesday nights because he was to see me Thursday morning.

The approach we used is called muscle setting, or working opposing muscle groups in the upper body. For instance, after warming up he'd start by pushing, doing bench presses to complete muscle failure. Then I'd take him to a back exercise that was a pulling motion, like rowing. Those pulling muscles had been relaxed, resting, while he was doing the pushing motion. We'd work them to failure.

We'd just go back and forth like that, and do the same thing with his legs. We'd go from machine to machine and lift weights that whole hour. We'd never stop. He really worked hard. I made him focus, think about what his muscles were doing. Slowed him down, made him feel the weights.

He's the best student I ever had. Very determined.

Garrett Boone:

Beck went through this incredible process of transforming his body from that of a mild-mannered pathologist to a world-class mountain climber. He had been a slight guy who spent a great deal of time indoors looking at slides. Over time, however, he transformed his chest and arms and legs. I've never seen anybody work as hard at anything in my whole life.

One of my favorite authors, Dan Jenkins, in his book *Baja Oklahoma,* outlined what he called "Mankind's Ten Stages of Drunkenness." I went over the top as a mountaineer when I achieved the final two stages, "Invisible" and "Bulletproof."

What I forgot was Jenkins's closing thought: "That last stage was about certain to end a marriage."

Meg:

He'd work out all day, and I'd never see him. Then he'd go and climb these mountains for weeks at a time. It was really kind of hard on me, just because I missed my dad and I wished he was here.

Bub:

I never really noticed when he was gone, because he was absent when he was here. He'd come home at six-thirty, eat, unwind and go to bed.

Peach:

Beck got up at four in the morning to exercise, and had to be in bed by eight o'clock at night. It was very boring. We had no social life.

Twenty-One

Cecilia Boone:

It was about this time that Beck decided Peach needed a passionate interest, that her life must be pretty flat, and that was why his mountain climbing bothered her so much. This was not a good approach for him to take.

Peach:

Beck was never available to do anything with me or the kids. It just didn't interest him. Then he started saying that I had to have a hobby, an interest. In other words, he felt I was unhappy because I wasn't doing anything fulfilling.

I discussed with Ken Zornes my thought that Peach would be happier if she had some interest that I could understand. She's a very bright and capable person. I thought that if she developed a passion it would also give me a better grasp of how she worked.

We weren't doing great. I thought she should know it was great by me if she had more opportunities to do things that stimulated her. Maybe that would bring us together.

Peach:

Or get Beck off the hook.

I thought about what he said, that I couldn't be happy just taking care of the kids. And I thought to myself, I've got to find something to make me happy. Then one day came a big realization. I *am* happy to be taking care of the kids. Leave me alone.

After that whenever he brought up the subject of hobbies for me I'd say, "Leave me alone. I'm perfectly happy. I don't consider myself to be a dull, dim person."

It was becoming increasingly difficult for me to focus on anything but climbing. By now, mountaineering was a full-blown obsession.

Two of the Seven Summits already were behind me, Elbrus and Aconcagua. At some point, I'd have to try Denali once more. Then besides Everest there was the Vinson Massif in Antarctica; Kilimanjaro in Africa and the Carstensz Pyramid in Irian Jaya, the Indonesian province on the west side of New Guinea.

The Carstensz Pyramid was a late-substitute addition to the

Seven Summits Quest. When Dick Bass first climbed them in the 1980s, Australia was represented by Mount Kosciusko, an unprepossessing 7,314-foot bump in New South Wales. In order to replace Kosciusko with a more worthy challenge—the Carstensz Pyramid—the Canadian photojournalist Pat Morrow (the second person after Dick Bass to complete the Seven Summits Quest) successfully lobbied to have Australia redefined as the Australo-Asian Tectonic Plate, or something like that, which subsumes New Guinea.

Of the five mountains I had yet to address, Everest was easily the toughest target, but the Vinson Massif and the Carstensz Pyramid presented unique and special problems, too. The former is the most physically remote and inaccessible of the seven summits, reachable only for a brief period of time around January each year, and then via a single expedition company. As I would discover, lots of things can go wrong on Antarctica.

The Carstensz Pyramid was a challenge of a different sort. At that particular time, Irian Jayans unhappy with their Indonesian overlords had formed into guerrilla groups and were considered a possible menace to the likes of me wanting to climb Carstensz—which they call Puncak Jaya, "Mount Victory."

So, I decided that my next major destination would be the bottom of the world.

Fun facts about Antarctica: At 5,100,000 square miles, it is the fifth largest continent after Asia, Africa and the Americas, and about twice the size of Australia. It has the highest average elevation of any continent, mainly because most of Antarctica is buried under about six thousand feet of ice. In some places the ice is more than two miles thick. No surprise, then, that Antarctica has the most fresh water (frozen, of course) of any continent. According to one estimate, if all that ice were to melt, the world's oceans would rise fifteen to twenty feet.

Adíos, Miami.

Yet Antarctica also has the driest climate on earth, much drier even than the Sahara.

Nothing the unaided eye would recognize as a living thing exists in the continental interior. Antarctica is a frozen desert. Its tallest peak, the 16,860-foot Vinson Massif (named for that intrepid Georgia congressman Carl G. Vinson) in the Ellsworth Mountains, wasn't identified until 1957, or climbed until 1966. At the time of my visit, January 1993, only fifteen previous expeditions—probably fewer than fifty people—had reached Vinson's summit.

"Antarctica," warned a brochure, "is one of the most inhospitable regions of the planet. The logistical problems are enormous, the weather highly unpredictable and tempestuous. Distances are immense, and facilities scarce. Safety and self-sufficiency are paramount concerns."

This is the list of gear I took for the climb:

For my feet:
  two pairs, light polypropylene socks
  two pairs, heavy polypropylene socks
  one pair Janus double boots with built-in supergaiter
    overboots
  Polar Guard booties

For my body:
  two pair light polypropylene underwear
  two pair expedition-weight polypropylene underwear
  one pair baggie shorts

Synchilla bibs
Marmot Gore-Tex bibs
Retropile jacket
Gore-Tex mountain shell
Marmot Alpinist down parka with hood

For my head:
one thick Synchilla balaclava
one neck gaiter
one ski hat
one bandanna
one fool's hat (This was my innovation. I figured if you're
   going to act like a fool, you might as well look like one.)
one sun hat
one face mask
two pairs of glasses
one pair UV-coated sunglasses
two ski goggles (two lenses) 100 percent UV and IR
   protection
two glasses straps
one antifog fluid
one glass-cleaning cloth
one set of earplugs

For my hands:
two pair expedition-weight polypropylene gloves
two pair of overmitts with liners and loops

Pack:
expedition backpack
sleeping bag—Marmot Penguin

one closed-cell foam pad
one Therm-A-Rest pad
vapor barrier liner

Technical equipment:
chest and seated harness
crampons—twelve-point
ice ax with wrist sling
ice hammer
two 6-millimeter prussic loops
three locking carabiners
four regular carabiners
one pair ski poles
one large duffel bag
rappel device
ascenders (pair) with slings
fixed rope sling
pack sling

Personal gear:
medical kit (including aspirin and Diamox)
sweatband
lip cream (SPF 15+)
sunblock (SPF 15+)
moleskin and second skin
large cup
large bowl
two spoons
three wide mouth water bottles with insulated covers
Swiss army knife

tube of hand cream
parachute cord
roll of duct tape
two Bic lighters
camera and film
several stuff sacks with nylon loops
reading books
toilet paper
shortwave radio
toilet kit
hard-candy snacks
garbage sacks
hand towel
money and tickets
water-purification tabs
Bactrim DS
Imodium
Pepto-Bismol tabs
Dalmane
freezer bags
mesh bags

The expedition began with a flight to Santiago, Chile, and then on to Punta Arenas, a community of approximately 100,000 situated at about 54 degrees south latitude on the Strait of Magellan in Chilean Patagonia. Punta Arenas sometimes is called the Earth's southernmost city.

Civilian access to Antarctica is strictly controlled. About the only way to get there is via Adventure Network International

(ANI), a Canadian-owned company formed in 1985. My guide, Martyn Williams of Santa Fe, New Mexico, was an ANI co-founder, along with Pat Morrow.

Besides our group heading for the Vinson Massif, ANI also was providing transportation and logistical support to three other expeditions on the ground, or rather ice, in Antarctica.

One was the American Women's Trans-Antarctic Expedition. These women brought parachutes with them, hoping that if the wind was right they could open them and skim along on their skis that way. That plan didn't work. They made it to the South Pole, but then had to return to Patriot Hills, the staging base in Antarctica for ANI.

Likewise, three Japanese adventurers trying to get to the South Pole didn't, and returned with frostbitten cheeks, a condition with which I'd later become familiar.

Then there was Erling Kagge, a thirtyish Norwegian whose fairly audacious plan was to cross from the coast to the South Pole alone and unaided on cross-country skis, making about forty or fifty kilometers a day. The staple of Kagge's diet was to be raw bacon, which has the highest caloric return of any kind of food. Bacon, at least theoretically, is ideal fuel for someone moving rapidly across a flat frozen expanse, dragging along behind him a sled weighing about 350 pounds. The trick, I was told, is to eat a little bit of bacon all the time. You cannot sit down to a big happy meal of it, even if you wanted to. Kagge kept his in a little pouch on his belt, and constantly chewed the stuff as he went along.

Eskimos, of course, eat blubber, which fires their engines in much the same way bacon did Kagge's. If you think that near the close of the millennium someone might have come up with something a bit more palatable, more high-tech than raw pork for Kagge, at least it sounds no worse than "hoosh," a vile melange that was the standard food for arctic explorers for decades. According to a recipe provided by Malcolm Browne in *The New York Times,* hoosh was a stew of seal or penguin meat, mixed with lard, flour, cocoa, sugar, salt and water. The tasteless freeze-dried mulch and cardboard I consumed on most of my mountain expeditions was ambrosia by comparison.

Kagge made it to the South Pole. He'd already conquered the North Pole. In 1994, he summited Everest with Rob Hall, and made a little bit of history by doing a live radio broadcast from the highest point on Earth.

Martyn Williams would be leading me and Barbara Gurtler, a petite and compact grandmother from St. Louis. There also were two other two-person expeditions joining us for the climb. One was the team of Charlotte Fox and Nola Royce, a school administrator and former competitive bodybuilder from upstate New York. They were in the care of Skip Horner, a Montanan who was the first person ever to guide all Seven Summits. Also on board was Sandy Pittman, who was climbing with a male friend, Chris Kinnen. Their guide was Pete Athans.

Punta Arenas is remote, and once you get there you still have about two thousand miles to go. Since it would be inordinately expensive for ANI to ship aviation fuel that far, the company must use airplanes capable of making the four thousand-mile round trip on one tank of kerosene.

The craft of choice in January of 1993 was a DC-6, which could make it to Patriot Hills and back in twelve hours, in perfect flying conditions. This is a meteorologically active part of the world, however, and a half day of perfect weather is difficult to guarantee. We got to know Punta Arenas quite well before finally taking off.

Everything connected with this particular adventure would be delayed and protracted, including the warfare between Peach and me that broke out in its aftermath.

After waiting for days to depart, there was the long flight to Patriot Hills, where the DC-6 disgorged us and immediately hightailed back to Chile. The abrupt leave-taking is absolutely necessary. If a storm comes up while the plane is on the ground, it likely never will leave. If anything goes wrong—such as a shift in the wind—on the way home on half a tank of fuel, a header into the Strait of Magellan is a distinct and unwelcome possibility.

Patriot Hills in January 1993 consisted of a couple of large tents and some ice tunnels dug for new arrivals, such as ourselves, who might require immediate shelter. There were no permanent aboveground structures. The tunnels also are used for storage. Because the weather at the time of our arrival was more or less clement, we put up our tents and built ice walls around them, just as I'd done on Denali.

Next morning, or what passed for morning—the antipodal summer sun stays above the horizon twenty-four hours a day—we all climbed into a twin-engine Otter for the two-hour flight to Base Camp at ten thousand feet on Vinson. It was very cold. We landed upslope, passed a sign that said, WELCOME TO VINSON BEACH and deplaned.

Once our tents were up, we needed to move a cache up to Camp One. You'll recall that my packing list didn't mention either skis or snowshoes, which both Barbara Gurtler and I had been assured we would not require. The snow was hard packed, we were told.

That was not true. Barbara, who is small and light, was not seriously inconvenienced. But I was heavy enough that with every step I created postholes above my knees. This made me seriously unhappy. We made our way up through some crevasses, dumped the stuff and returned. Everyone else shussed down the hill in about two seconds. It took me forever. Thirty hours after taking off, we finally had dinner and went to sleep.

I believe it was the next morning that I clambered out of my tent and was stunned to see three identical suns suspended in the sky above us. I knew nothing until that moment of sun dogs, in which a layer of ice in the atmosphere reflects an image of the sun onto multiple points in the sky.

The additional suns lent the already surreal landscape an even more unworldly cast. I was very much reminded of the opening scenes of *Star Wars*, and the multiple suns over Luke Skywalker's home planet.

It was in the mess tent where I first encountered Rob Hall— in the form of a poster for the guide service he'd begun with his then-partner and close friend Gary Ball. They called themselves Hall and Ball. It sounded like a rock band.

I was deeply impressed to learn that Hall and Ball had managed to climb all seven summits in just seven months, an incredible logistical feat that culminated where I was standing, the Vinson Massif, on December 12, 1990.

In October of 1993, Gary Ball would succumb to cerebral edema—HACE—high on 26,795-foot Dhaulagiri in the Himalayas, the world's sixth tallest mountain. Rob Hall was in the tent to hold his friend as he fell into a coma, and then buried Gary Hall the next day in a crevasse.

Our first day of climbing we were out in our T-shirts and made it to High Camp across a small ice field in good shape. Next day, however, the leading edge of a storm system reached us before we could summit, driving the entire group back down to High Camp. We tried, and succeeded, on our second march to the top, which proved anticlimactic. All we found up there was a ski pole stuck in the ground. The view from the top of Vinson reportedly is spectacular. I'll never know; my glasses were fogged over. We couldn't see squat anyway. Everything was gray. Then the weather started to deteriorate. My return to Base Camp was done blind, more or less, just as I'd been blind on the way down from Denali. I managed to set a new world's record for falling into crevasses. I dropped into five of them on that single day.

The Otter came to fetch us on schedule, but by the time it arrived the weather had gone to pieces at Patriot Hills, which meant the pilot and his mechanic were stuck. They tossed out their beds and tents and set up housekeeping with the rest of us—the metal inside the plane would make it feel much colder than in the tents—and waited for the weather to improve. It didn't for a couple of days.

We were forced to excavate old food caches at Base Camp, some frozen eggs and vegetables that had been there for ages. Sandy Pittman, I recall, had this enormous bag of gourmet food:

seaweed salad, smoked duck and the damnedest other delicacies, as well as a video camera with which she could play movies in her tent. She did share *some* of her luxuries with the group. But Sandy, who was generally a good sport and able expedition member, also had a bottle of Jack Daniel's, which she would *not* share with me no matter how long I stood outside her tent with my little tin cup.

Otherwise very little transpired out there in the middle of nowhere, except that Barbara Gurtler contrived to set our mess tent on fire. She incorrectly started up the stove, which flamed up the side of the tent, sending us all either diving into the snow outside, or putting the fire out.

The miniconflagration aside, Barbara was generally appalled at our cooking conditions. Martyn, for example, prepared what he called a lying dinner; he cooked up anything he found lying around.

At this point, I made a connection with one of the great mountaineers of this century, Reinhold Messner. As we excavated the old food caches, we came across a pack of chocolate pudding inscribed with Messner's name. He'd been there years before. The way I see it, at least at some level Reinhold and I have dined together.

Deep into the second day of our frozen exile, thick clouds descended all around us, a worrisome development. We discovered at the same time that the Otter was frozen to the ice. We tried rocking the plane, and prying it loose with shovels. Just as local visibility was about to hit zero we broke the plane free, jumped in and headed back to Patriot Hills, where the DC-6 would retrieve us for the return flight to Punta Arenas.

At least that was the plan.

On its way from Chile, the big plane blew an engine and turned back. Working D-6 replacement engines never are as plentiful as you'd like them to be—the nearest available one was found in Florida—so we had no choice but to chill our heels the week or eight days it took to get the big bird safely airborne again.

Nola Royce:

They had a solar-powered radio set up at Patriot Hills. It could reach Punta Arenas. When we discovered we were going to be stuck for a while, we all gave names of family and friends who needed to be told why we were delayed. These were supposed to be relayed on from Punta Arenas. Some people don't understand that you can't just pick up a telephone when you are out in the middle of nowhere.

I don't know how many calls got through, but mine didn't. My aunt in New York was just frantic to find out what had happened to me, just absolutely frantic. Nobody contacted her.

Peach:

When Beck went off on these trips, he'd never call home to check on us. He would go for weeks without communicating.

I was used to that. What I wasn't prepared for was to go to the airport to pick him up and find he wasn't on the plane. I was totally undone by this.

I called the tour operator. They told me that he must be all right, because if he were dead I already would have been contacted! Then I called a travel agent friend, who informed me that someone had canceled Beck's reservation home. It was days before I knew about the blown engine on the DC-6, and that Beck was all right.

This incident was a turning point.

Pat White:

I remember how terrified Peach was. For several days she didn't know where the hell he was, how he was or whether he was dead or alive. It was a terrible foretaste of what she'd go through when she was told he'd died on Everest. I waited with her until she heard something. We all just had knives in our stomachs. Peach swore she wouldn't go through that again. I saw her anger and determination.

We weren't in any danger at Patriot Hills, but there also wasn't much to do while we were waiting for the DC-6 to be fixed. So some of us helped out on a project. ANI owned a single-engine Cessna, which the company kept year-round at Patriot Hills. In the past, their practice had been to excavate a hole in the ice and snow and then to ease the plane down into it, nose first. Then they'd fill up the hole, leaving a bit of the Cessna's tail showing so they could locate the plane the following summer.

This year, we created sort of a subsurface ice grotto into which we carefully lowered the airplane backward, and then fitted the cavity with a plywood ceiling and ramp so that the Cessna was both protected and could be easily wheeled out for use the next year.

We had just finished—Patriot Hills was beginning to feel like a penal colony—when the DC-6 hove into view, ready to whisk yours truly back to Peach's side. When I did finally land in Dallas, an unseasonable chill had descended; the drive back home from the airport was not cordial. Peach informed me we were going to see a marriage counselor.

Meg, Beck, Peach and
Beck II, fall 1999.

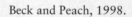

Beck and Peach, 1998.

Howard Olson.

PART FOUR

Twenty-Two

Peach:
I don't think Beck had a clue of the distress this episode caused me. My hair started falling out, and I lost about forty pounds over a three-month period.

In most of our conversations, if you could call them that, she beat on me incessantly. I'd never seen anybody fight. My parents never fought. So when Peach showed her anger, I'd withdraw, which made her feel even worse. She'd come back at me even harder.

Eventually I'd get thoroughly ticked off and we'd argue. But mostly I'd be silent. She'd come right out and say what bothered her. I just could not do that. I wasn't very good at it at all. I'd shut down—withdraw. My stomach would go into knots for days. And we'd just keep going over the same territory.

Meg:

Luckily, our parents did not include my brother or me in this. I only remember one mountain-climbing discussion. There was a lot of tension. My mother said something like "If you climb another mountain I'll divorce you." Then they both noticed that I'd come into the room and they didn't say anything else.

Bub:

It wasn't a family topic. They talked about it on their own time. Obviously, there was some tension, but I didn't choose sides. Nor did either one of them try to make us choose sides.

Linda Gravelle:

Peach and Beck kept their differences to themselves. She came to us, her friends, when she needed to talk, but you never felt any conflict in the Weathers house. Peach is very good at making people feel at home. She set the emotional tone of the household, and Beck followed.

Peach:

We went to dinner one time with Beck's parents, and afterward I played with his head a little bit. I asked, "Why do you never disagree with your parents on any issue?"

He answered, "I can't disagree with them out of love and respect. You just don't do that."

I kept digging at him. "Well, Beck," I said, "how are they ever going to know what you really think?"

He didn't respond. Not long afterward, Beck and his mother

got into a humongous political argument. I think it was over President Clinton. I left the room, but our son stayed to listen. Later he told me, "Mama, I felt so sorry for Mimi"—my children call their grandmother Weathers Mimi—"because Daddy just pounded her."

I said, "Don't feel sorry. He's doing this because he can't tell her that he doesn't want a red sweater. He's her product."

I didn't understand why we couldn't manage to be more happy together, given that we had no external problems. We had great kids. My work was going fine. We didn't have any grand debts. There were none of the obvious kinds of triggers that get people at each other.

Peach:

The second counselor we went to was as useless as the first.

After we'd talked at length, over several weeks, about Beck withdrawing from the family, physically and emotionally, he said, "Well, there are people who don't need people, who just like to be by themselves. I think Beck's one of those."

That did us absolutely no good. The truth of the matter is that there's something wrong with people who stay by themselves. That's why we call them loners. I didn't understand why this guy couldn't see that Beck was depressed.

As I'm sitting there with my hair falling out, he went on. "You need to share. You need to share and unload on each other." Looking across the desk at him, I was thinking, "I believe you are not even in the same universe with us."

If anything, this guy reinforced me. He certainly said it was okay for me to take off. "Follow your own heart! Go for the dream." Great!

Peach:

That week of fearing and not knowing if Beck was alive or dead was a watershed in a couple of ways. The mountaineering went from something I disliked to something that I hated. A part of me felt, If he cared about the kids and me at all, how could he possibly do this? Beck contended that he loved us, and it never occurred to me that he couldn't love the kids. Maybe me, but not them.

The other part of this was that he would neither release us nor embrace us. From Antarctica forward, it would have been real easy for him to get a divorce. Real easy.

I made some changes. I stopped blaming myself for our problems and started putting the blame where it belonged. I now saw that what Beck was doing was simply unfair. Oddly, I had always been the trusting one. Never had any reason not to be. Beck, of course, never trusted anyone. But after Antarctica that changed. I better take care of myself, I thought, because no one else is going to.

I became self-contained. It really wasn't that difficult. I just planned my own schedule.

One of my pet delusions at this time was that no matter how bad it got with Peach, it would be okay once I'd gone to Everest, whether or not I got to the top. I'd be okay, and everything could return to normal. In all honesty, if I'd summited Everest, I would have zipped right back and bombed up and down McKinley. I would not have been able to leave the Seven undone. That would have been too close. But at that point, I would not have climbed again. I sincerely believed that. I also believed we still could make the marriage work. I'd never divorce Peach. If we were split up, she'd have to do it. I still loved her, and there was no way I'd give up my children.

Twenty-Three

Peach:

Part of the reason Beck climbed mountains was that he craved attention. There are some people who do things very quietly. You really have to extract information from them. With Beck, it was about the only thing he'd talk about.

There was working out, the next climb, what you were going to do, where you were going to go. At cocktail parties, whatever the subject, he'd bring the conversation around to what his next little project might be. You could almost see peoples' eyes roll back into their heads as they tried to get away from him.

It is boring to hear people talk about themselves. Beck didn't catch that. Beck did not read other people. He wasn't aware of their feelings.

Terry White:

I think some people were truly interested when he started talking about it. I'm not sure they still were after an hour. Of course, if you get Beck started on *anything* you can get at least half an hour. Pap smears, for example, are a subject he can go on about at length—and does.

Pat White:

It's not like Beck to brag. I think he was really engrossed in it. I remember one time at a party, I was mad at him for being so stupid. Then he started talking about climbing. I got caught up in it. He was describing something that most of us don't have the chance to experience. It was spellbinding, because he is a good storyteller. I got sucked in despite myself. I could see the allure for him. I could see how the mountains could pull him. I guess I forgave him a little bit.

The Carstensz Pyramid, named for a Dutch navigator who first spied the peak, is a thirty-pitch rock climb, not a high-grade technical challenge.

There are areas of exposure, sort of like the step you do on Longs Peak, from the east face to the north face. You have to let go of something, and just sort of step out straight into the void to make a long and very committing step to another wall. Otherwise, the only problem is rain, which can considerably heighten any climb's degree of difficulty.

Irian Jaya, an Indonesian province since the 1960s, is among the least explored corners of the Earth. There are large portions of the New Guinea highlands that are described on maps only as "obscured by clouds." It wasn't until fairly recently that everyone finally agreed the Carstenz Pyramid is 16,500 feet (more or less) tall.

Our November 1994 expedition was led by Skip Horner. We flew to the little island of Biak, near Irian Jaya, and then over to New Guinea itself, where we spent one night in the town of Nabire. Since we were near sea level and only a couple of degrees off the equator, it was very hot, but not as humid as Katmandu.

Accommodations in Nabire were not modern. We had running water only in the sense that our bathrooms were outfitted with vats that you filled from a cold water tap. You showered by dipping a bucket in your vat, which drained through a hole in the floor and out into an open sewer. The same hole in the floor served as your toilet.

A trip to secure some cash turned out to be a novel experience. Apparently, counterfeiting is a major industry in that part of the world, so that money handlers are keenly vigilant to avoid accepting bogus bills.

The local bank we tried to patronize would accept only crisp, new notes. If the paper money you handed them to exchange appeared ever to have been put to its intended use, they wouldn't accept it. Breaking a U.S. $50 bill required an hour of patient waiting as various people walked in and out of the room to stare at the note, turn it over, ponder its authenticity.

From Nabire we flew in a chartered plane back in time to Ilaga, a little airfield on a jungle plateau adjacent to the village of Dani. One of several New Guinean Stone Age tribes, the Dani go barefoot, wear penis gourds and grass skirts and bones in their noses—reputedly, they once were ritual cannibals—and appear to have descended down a very straight family tree.

Every kid had some sort of upper-respiratory infection, and as far as I could tell the national bird was the fly.

Not a lot seemed to go on in the village, so we were a welcome diversion. They were fascinated by anything electronic. A chance to look over a wristwatch with an LCD readout was like a ticket to the Super Bowl for them. The kids would walk up one at a time and stare at my arm and then wander off. It was the neatest thing they'd ever seen.

About forty of the Dani had gone ahead with our gear, which they carried on their heads. It would take them a week to get to the mountain through some very rough jungle terrain; we would cover the same distance, three at a time, in a helicopter we shared with a group led by Rob Hall. I recognized the lanky New Zealander from the picture of him I'd seen in Antarctica, and was immediately impressed with his considerable organizational and logistical skills. Under his overall management, this trip flowed together seamlessly. It should have required three to four weeks; we'd easily complete our objective—door-to-door—in two.

I was even more impressed later on, however, when I observed Hall's constant concern for safety. He took great precautions in establishing our route. I quickly grew confident in Rob's leadership abilities.

Yasuko Namba was along as well. Although the language barrier prevented us from exchanging much more than basic pleasantries, she seemed a fit and well-experienced mountaineer.

It was a two-day walk from Base Camp to where we actually began the climb, at about ten thousand feet. The first night we camped in a pretty little meadow. The Dani porters found themselves a cave and cut down a bunch of trees, which they lit on fire at its entrance, turning the cave into a sort of meat smoker. I can't imagine what they were doing in there, or how they handled the thick smoke.

Two interesting things happened the next day. A wolf ran out on the trail. One of the Dani whipped out his bow and arrow and dropped the wolf in midstride, a hell of a shot. Then he and the rest of them fell on the animal and ate it raw. They didn't grab chunks of wolf in their teeth, snarl at each other and run in different directions, but they did consume the animal right there and then. They wolfed him down.

I was beginning to get a sense of how tough these guys are, masters of their environment, dressed in little more than their smiles. I, by contrast, felt like an effete, privileged weenie. Despite all our high-tech gear, we could not have been more completely out of place there. Also, now that I'd seen how the Dani behave when they're hungry, I was effusively polite for the rest of the trip. I figured if nothing else, they'd eat me last.

The one thing you don't want to be around the Dani is Indonesian. Whether the government in Jakarta is trying to populate Irian Jaya with its own pioneers—in which case the native tribes get shoved aside—or is dealing harshly with civil insurrection, Dani villages have been strafed and Indonesians are not well liked there. One of our guides on this trip was an Indonesian who on a prior outing made the mistake of being caught alone with the locals. They chased him for about five miles. Since the Dani all were carrying knives, there was no doubt in his mind what they intended to do if they captured him.

The second singularity of the day came as we climbed above

the tree line. Displayed along the trail at the top of the pass was a human skull. The previous owner was unknown. Perhaps a Dani, or a slow-footed Indonesian. For us, it was a stark reminder that not everyone who takes this trail returns.

Rob Hall's group summited first, then we went up and down. At about thirteen thousand or fourteen thousand feet I experienced a little surprise—my vision shifted. It wasn't anything dramatic. Although my reading glasses suddenly were useless, my eyesight didn't blur. It just was a little different. Since there was no mention of this problem anywhere in the literature about radial keratotomy, I assumed it was a minor and inconsequential side effect of my recent operation. I had no inkling of the crisis I'd encounter at the really high altitude and low light on Mount Everest.

The precipitating cause for undergoing the procedure had occurred in New Hampshire on an ice climb with Steve Young. By then I had tried everything; prescription goggles, hard contacts, goggles with little fans in them, soft contacts, semisoft contacts. Nothing worked.

In New Hampshire, I was trying to scale about thirty feet of totally vertical ice, working hard and starting to sweat. My glasses iced over from the steam off my face until I couldn't see where I was going. Finally, I fell, and was suspended from the ice by a single wrist loop. My face was smack up against this vertical wall of ice, and I couldn't see where to put my feet.

Young, who had me belayed, laughed at me as I took my ax in the opposite hand and flailed away at the wall until I actually penetrated the ice surface with the tool, then dug in my front point crampon knives. I screamed with each step, until I finally got to the top. At that point I decided, Okay, I'm going to have my eyes operated on.

Peach:

Beck was not a candidate for RK surgery. He couldn't find anybody in Medical City to do it. If you're really nearsighted, as he is, a deeper cut is needed, which means you'll get more fluctuation when you go up in altitude. He had it done anyway.

People knew that laser surgery was on the horizon. I talked to Beck about that. I asked, "Why don't you wait six months? This new stuff that's coming up is much better. It doesn't weaken your eyes." He said, "No."

I think he'd tell you he wouldn't do it again.

A drenching rain broke over the Carstensz Pyramid just as we got back to High Camp. Skip Horner, who had hung back to take down some of our gear, was caught in the deluge, which turned the mountain's upper slopes into a waterfall. Luckily, Horner made it back to camp intact.

We all then retraced the path to Base Camp, where the helicopter flew us back to the Dani village. We spent the night in their grass huts. Wondering what sort of health hazard such overnight accommodations might present, some guys decided to sleep out in their tents.

Before the charter came for us the next day, I watched a bunch of Dani children playing soccer, or their version of the sport. There were no goals, and instead of a proper soccer ball they used a ratty old tennis ball. Like the adults, the kids were more or less naked.

One of them had only one leg and a stick—no crutch. But he was hell-bent for leather, and none of the others cut him any slack. The whole group was just having the time of their lives, laughing and running around in the dirt. They were sweet kids. It occurred to me how impossible a sight such as this would be in North Dallas.

Twenty-Four

In 1994 I again inflamed Peach by purchasing a big, fast motorcycle, a Honda ST 1100 touring bike. I called her Scarlett O'Honda. Peach just loathed Scarlett. I doubt there is anything I could have done to make my wife any angrier. The motorcycle was such a divisive issue between us that the mere mention of Scarlett provokes Peach to this day.

We cannot even agree on the exact circumstances surrounding Scarlett's acquisition, except that I bugged and bugged her about it, over time, and took the occasion of Peach and the kids' absence from town to pick up my shiny new beast. I remember that she finally gave in to my intense lobbying. That's not Peach's recollection.

Peach:

Had it been just the mountain climbing, including Everest, matters might have been different. But if he thought I hated something, he did it. There were the guns, and then the motorcycle. Apparently it is typical for depressed people to lash out against those to whom they are closest. He was rubbing my face in it pretty good.

Motorcycles were just another one of those things in my life that I enjoyed, lost interest in, then came back to later. I had the Vespa in high school, then a Suzuki when I was a resident. I got rid of the Suzuki when I realized I was getting a little reckless with it. I always enjoyed driving them fast. But this was unconnected to the depression.

Peach:

It absolutely was connected to the depression.

I had just about decided that I'd put up with the mountain climbing after all when he brought this thing into the house.

I hated it.

I said, "If you get a motorcycle, I'm going to get a new car." I'm not a big car person. I'm happy to drive whatever I have for six or seven years. So he did, and I did. He didn't care, and I didn't feel any better. I liked my new car, but I didn't feel any better.

Scarlett wasn't just a motorcycle. It was real fast and powerful, one more way for him to get away from us. For instance, when we went to the beach, instead of driving with the kids and me he rode his motorcycle. He ended up spending a day with us, then rode his motorcycle back.

That motorcycle also had too many bells and whistles. The

battery would go dead. There was *always* something wrong with it. Finally, he said he would sell it, but he didn't. He had a million reasons why he couldn't. So I knew it was going to be mine to get rid of. There was nothing that I hated worse, but I knew with amazing clarity that it would be mine to deal with.

Mount Kilimanjaro didn't enter my plans until I began seriously considering the Seven Summits Quest, leading up to the Everest climb. Kilimanjaro may be among the better known mountains in the world, and, at 19,340 feet, it is tall enough to make trouble for the unwary, especially those who do not take sufficient time to acclimatize themselves. Still, Kilimanjaro is not really a climb. It is a good hard hike on which you encounter lots of amateurs.

I went to Africa near the end of December 1995 with a group led once again by Skip Horner. We flew into Nairobi, and then drove to the trailhead in Tanzania. There, we met our group of porters—mostly males, but a few females, too—led by a genial fellow named Genesis.

Besides performing the usual porter tasks of humping our gear up the mountain and making and breaking camp, Genesis's team also sang. As far as I know, they are the world's only singing porters (the Dani chanted), a true a cappella choir who'd mastered a range of tunes in their native tongue (Swahili, I think), including some original compositions. They sang them for us in a series of daytime concerts. I enjoyed that a lot.

I did not enjoy much else. As we crossed the broad grassy

plain that gradually slopes up to Kilimanjaro proper, I was taken with the usual mountaineer's crud: vomiting, aches, etc. Although its cause forever will remain a mystery, my best guess is that the cooking got me.

My salvation was a doc on the trip who'd luckily brought along an antiemetic—basically a heavy tranquilizer—that stunned me into an extended slumber from which I awoke feeling pretty awful.

As I dressed that morning, Skip Horner accosted me with the mountain guide's signature soft solicitude, saying, "You may not enjoy this, but you are going to go to the top." He was right all around. After a three-day hike up a gentle grade, we rested and then made the usual midnight assault to the top of Mount Kilimanjaro, Uhuru Peak.

I now was poised for Mount Everest, which I was scheduled to climb that spring. The mountain had been on my mind for at least four years, ever since Aconcagua, but I wanted to correctly prepare for it. In my view, it would have been presumptuous to climb, say, Denali, and maybe one other mountain and then go to Everest. The Seven Summits are not just about summits. For me, they also were about process and people and being part of that world.

Following the 1994 expedition to Carstensz Pyramid, I called Skip Horner and asked him who he thought was the best Everest guide. He said he thought Rob Hall was probably the most experienced guide on the mountain. I contacted Rob and asked to be included in the 1996 climb. He welcomed me aboard.

Nineteen ninety six was an important year for me. I turned fifty that year, and had read somewhere that you shouldn't expect to climb supertall mountains much after that age. You start getting into physiologic problems. You're on the downhill side of the power curve. I realized that I was losing just a little bit of edge every year, that I didn't have quite the same level of strength and endurance. The window was closing on me.

Outside of work and sleep, about all I had done for five years was exercise and climb. My life had taken on a monastic quality. Now, with the Everest climb just five months away, I stepped up my conditioning program.

Peach:

The first I ever heard about Everest came at a restaurant in Dallas where Beck and I were eating hamburgers. An acquaintance, John Hazleton, came up and congratulated Beck on being accepted on the expedition. My teeth nearly dropped out. Not only had I known nothing of this, I also was unaware of what it would cost: $65,000.

What made this news all the more disturbing to me was that Bub was about to go on a wilderness adventure of his own, a school expedition to the mountains of West Texas, which had me very concerned. This was an annual event. On a recent trip one of the boys suffered pulmonary edema, the same condition I believe my husband developed on Denali. I knew it was dangerous, and I wondered how well equipped the leaders of this outing were to deal with such emergencies. From the evidence, not very.

By this time, nearly three years after Antarctica, I'd grown accustomed to leading my life separate from Beck. We all still resided under the same roof when he was in town, but he and I were intimate strangers.

When he was gone, I refused to stay at home, the mountaineering widow and her brood. So, for example, when Beck went to Kilimanjaro, I took the kids to New York and had a great time with them. I certainly wasn't going to wait for people to invite me over to their house because they felt sorry for me.

I never exercised fewer than five days a week, and had been getting out of bed for my workouts at four or four-thirty every morning, six days a week, for five years. My schedule with Brent was three one-hour sessions a week—all strength work—alternating with three days when I concentrated on endurance and aerobics. These sessions usually started with the lower-body cross-training machine. Then I moved to the revolving staircase for thirty minutes before finishing up on the recumbent bike, also for thirty minutes. Sundays were the only days I didn't work out.

Now I added an hour of aerobics on strength days, plus an extra half hour on aerobic days in the morning, and another hour in the afternoon. This required patronizing two different gyms.

I did not take any vitamins or minerals or supplements, or pay particular attention to what I ate. I was on the see-food diet. If you see food, you eat it. In this way, I finally built myself up from the 150 pounds I weighed when I started climbing to 180 pounds, where I wanted to be.

Pat White:

Peach was not happy about Beck going to Everest. I remember that my husband and other people worried that Beck might get frostbitten again. But the joke was "That's nothing. Wait till he gets home and Peach takes a bite out of his ass for being that stupid."

Peach:

I tried to get him to talk to the kids. I said, "You need to talk to them in case something happens to you and you don't come back." He didn't do that. When I asked him for power of attorney, he became furious. I said, "It's not a choice."

Meg:

When I found out he was going to climb Mount Everest, I felt a little betrayed. I sat him down here in the house after he came back from Kilimanjaro. I said, "Please, please, don't go. It's way too dangerous!"

He said, "The death rate on Mount Everest is not that high."

I suppose that's true for people who don't even make it to Camp Two. But I'd read somewhere that a lot of people who make it to the top don't make it back down. I really didn't want him to be there. He didn't give me a satisfactory explanation.

I didn't believe anything was going to happen to me. I truly believed I was going to go away for a few weeks and come back intact. The whole problem would disappear. I discounted Meg's fears because I was so sure nothing would happen to me.

Cecilia Boone:

We went over to their house the night before Beck left for Everest, to tell him good-bye and to wish him well. Peach was in the bedroom and would not come out.

Garrett Boone:

The two kids were there. In front of us, he kept telling them this was going to be okay. It wasn't dangerous. Rob Hall was the best out there. He'd planned everything very conservatively. It was going to be fine. I didn't listen to what he was saying so much as why he was saying it. The kids obviously were worried about their father being away and their mother being so upset.

Cecilia Boone:

He was talking to us, but clearly the message was for the children, too.

Pat White:

Just before he went to Everest, we had a coffee meeting. Peach was very conflicted. She said it was hard to go to the airport with him. She said, "I'm angry, but at the same time I'm terrified something might happen. You don't want to send someone you love out to face peril having chewed their ass off. You want to hug them and tell them you love them."

Terry White:

The people who know Beck did not require he become a mountain climber in order for us to enjoy him as a human being, and to respect him. This was his need, not his friends' need. He didn't need to do this for us. About six weeks before he went to Everest I sat down in his office and closed the door and told him he didn't need to do this to prove to me that he was my friend. If he didn't go that was fine with me. I think he was surprised, and I think he appreciated it. But I don't know how much it slowed him down. It was probably something I should have said sooner.

I don't remember my exact response to Terry, but in essence it was "I appreciate what you're telling me. But I want to do this. I'm prepared to do it." I was touched by what Terry said. Most people do not have the courage to stand up and say, "Deny your dream. No one will blame you."

In part, I was going because I had something to prove to myself. But at this late moment, I might as well have been jumping off a cliff. You maybe reconsider the idea on the way down, but there's no turning back.

Twenty-Five

When I came off the mountain, I first had to deal with what I was, and where I was. One of the odd twists to this story was that nobody—including me—knew how badly I was injured. First I was dead. Then I wasn't. Then I might as well have been dead. Then came Madan K.C. and the helicopter rescue. I wouldn't know the whole unhappy truth of my medical condition for weeks.

All the photographs I'd ever seen of frostbite were of horribly swollen and blistered hands. At the clinic in Katmandu, my hands were cold and the gray color of a piece of meat that's been left in a leaky freezer bag for a couple of years. But there was no swelling, gross discoloration or blistering. I knew what frostbite was. When the tips of my fingers were frostbitten on Denali, it was *really* painful. This time there was no pain at all.

Except in my psyche. It was humbling at the Yak & Yeti to discover they'd stationed some guy outside my door to come and wipe my ass if necessary. I'd go without eating for a week to avoid something like that, which practically was the case, in any event.

Fortunately, Dan showed up. Then we went out to eat something. We found a lovely little restaurant in the hotel, a beautiful setting, and right off the bat I realized they didn't know what to do with me. How were they going to serve me?

I had to find something on the menu you could eat with a spoon, and even then Dan had to feed me. I was not thrilled with that.

Then there were other people's responses: the Nepalese official who stared me up and down; the housekeeper who dropped her mop. I was beginning to see how it feels to be a freak.

But I still didn't sense what a disaster had occurred.

Back home in Dallas, where Terry White oversaw my medical needs, it was arranged for me to meet the hand surgeon, Mike Doyle. He asked me to spread my fingers, make a fist and cross my fingers on both hands, all of which I was able to do.

Mike said, "You're probably going to lose most of your fingers on your right hand, and the tips of your fingers on the left. We need to get a scan done so we can look at the vessels."

He called me later that day. I could tell he was really upset. "I don't know how to tell you this," he began, "but you don't have any blood supply in your right hand. It stops above the wrist. And you have very little in your left hand. I don't know what to say."

My frostbite was so severe that no vessels were functioning. They had frozen in place and filled with thrombosed coagulate. The reason I hadn't seen any edema or swelling was that they were completely dead: no vessels, no fluid.

This was a terrible surprise. I basically had a set of dead puppets. I was still (temporarily) able to pull the strings on them, because the controlling tendons extended into my forearms. But my hands were as good as gone.

My son, Beck, and his friend Charles White went to work on the TV remote control, gluing little paddles of wood to it so I could press the buttons. I was both touched and immeasurably saddened by that gesture.

We have a bright friend, Yolanda Brooks, who advises businesses on how to make their buildings handicap accessible. She brought by the books showing how to type with your teeth, and a whole range of other such devices, each page a testament to my inability to take care of myself.

There were some grimly funny moments. I remember sitting in a chair when a big chunk of my right eyebrow, hair included, fell off in my hand. Later, as I was walking down the hall, my left big toe broke off and went skittering away.

Our lamps were an interesting surprise. They turn on and off at a human touch. Of course, when I touched them with my dead hands, nothing happened.

I did try to see if we could get something back in my hands. I went to hydrotherapy twice a day, seven days a week. I did all the exercises. But all I was doing was working my dead puppets.

As you do that, you notice your fingers, one by one, start turning to stone. One day you can bring one of them all the way down. Next day, halfway. Next day it'll wiggle a little bit. Next day, nothing. Gradually you watch them solidify, quit working, start to shrink and then mummify.

At my wrists you could see the demarcation between living

and dead tissue, where my body was trying to shed its dead member. It can actually do that with something small, like a finger or toe. But with something big like a wrist and hand, you have to cut it off.

Of course, my nose had been frozen, too, and would fall off. But I wasn't really worried about my face at that point. I figured the worst that could happen there was I'd just be incredibly ugly. It did bother me, though, that I had to tie a pork chop around my neck to get the dog to play with me.

My hands were a different story.

My brother Kit showed up at some point, and one time went with me to a hydrotherapy session.

"Wouldn't it be great," he said, "if we could get a fake hand, paint it black and then dump it in the rolling water? Then you stick your hand under your arm and scream, 'My hand fell off!' " I thought it was a pretty funny idea, and I would have done it if Kit could have found a fake hand.

During this same period, I was trying to preserve my independence, even while I was surrendering to my helplessness, which was an inescapable reality. As much as I didn't want Dan wiping my fanny, I *hated* for Peach to do it.

Peach also oversaw my showers. We only tried a tub bath once. Everything went smoothly enough until I tried to get out, and realized I was too weak to do so. I thought for a moment that we'd have to drain the water and then call on some friends to drag me up over the edge of the tub so I could stand.

After quite a while I actually managed to get to my feet. Thereafter, when we needed to wash my hair, I'd get a small stool to crawl up on the counter by the kitchen sink. There I knew I at least could roll off the counter to get back to the floor.

Peach:

I never said anything, but there was a lot of tacit "I told you so" in this period.

There was self-recrimination. Not really over going to Everest. That *was*. As bizarre as this sounds, there was some recompense in having gotten myself nearly killed in a famous place. It made it easier. It's different than being mangled in an industrial accident, or sticking your finger in a light socket.

I had survived, which was concrete, and a contrast to those folks who didn't. That helps keep you going. After hearing me tell my story before an audience, a very famous American astronaut once said to me, "You must have had a horseshoe right up your ass that day." Yessir. I know that.

Ultimately, things like helping out on the IMAX film of the expedition, which I did while my hands were still wrapped up, also were therapeutic. You're not just sitting in your room, staring at the wall.

Yet the truth of my situation was brought home in unexpected ways. We had a party for Meggie at an arcade not far from our house. There was another party for smaller children—seven or eight years old—going on. These kids would come running by, see me, and stop in midstride, almost as if they were struck dumb.

Each such incident reinforced my awareness of just how much I'd changed, and how different I was from everybody else.

About the only significant physical pain I felt at this time was the infection in my right arm. It was red and swollen, and each day you could see the infection advancing up my upper arm. It took a number of tries before we found an antibiotic with the power to stop it.

With all my various infections, I would stay on a steady antibiotic regimen for more than a year. Every time I tried to stop, I'd pus out somewhere and have to start taking the antibiotics again.

The real agonies hadn't yet begun. The joke later would be that I underwent so many surgeries over the next year (eleven in all) that the doctors didn't waste time sewing me up. They just put in zippers. Actually, there was a kernel of truth to the joke. I proved allergic to the surgical tape that covered nearly every part of me at one time or another. So on top of everything else, there was the indignity of having my skin blister and slough off under my bandages even as the rest of me was being sawn, snipped and sliced away, bit by bit.

Mike Doyle found a reconstructive plastic surgeon for me, Greg Anigian, who would operate to save whatever function possible in my ravaged left hand. Greg later rebuilt my destroyed nose, too. Reconstructive plastic surgeons—"dirty" plastic surgeons, in hospital parlance—are very different from their colleagues who specialize in cosmetic plastic surgery. They are not vanity engineers. What they do is big-time stuff, and they tend to be fantastic at it. The better ones can sew a fart to a moonbeam. I'd put Greg among them, even if he is an Aggie from Texas A&M.

The surgical strategy we agreed upon would place me under general anesthesia for sixteen hours as Doyle and Anigian cut and stitched away. Mike's part was comparatively straightforward. Had there been anything left of my right wrist, we might have considered fitting me with some high-tech device, or at least trying to preserve as much tissue as possible against the day that truly advanced bionic technology would become available.

But since no part of the wrist was salvageable, the decision was simple: just trim the limb up to where my arm was the right length for a low-tech prosthesis, such as the one I now wear. This was what I called the nineteenth-century, or Civil War, side of my surgery. It was essentially a battlefield amputation.

The other side was twenty-first-century work: multistep, complex and time consuming, not to mention risky. Greg Anigian would perform microsurgery and tinker with tiny vessels. Thrombosis and more dead tissue were a real concern. I did not want double stumps.

One of the first things I noticed when I came out of this surgery was that they'd strapped a fetal Doppler monitor on me—the kind of device usually attached to pregnant women's bellies—to keep a close watch on my hand's circulation.

Anigian had a little of my thumb and most of my palm to work with. For raw materials, he harvested a length of fascia from the left side of my head, a piece of the left latissimus dorsi muscle (and its blood supply) from my back and a generous swath of skin from my left side.

He wrapped the muscle tissue around my stump and hooked it up to the radial artery. Then he attached the fascia around my thumb and sewed it to an artery, too. Finally, he wrapped the whole thing up in skin from my side, creating a sort of mitt for me.

Dan:

I was waiting for Beck in the recovery room after his surgery. He'd been extubated, which means they'd removed the tube inserted in his trachea to help him breathe.

I don't recall ever seeing anyone in so much pain. He was shaking uncontrollably. Although he still was markedly drugged, Beck was suffering major-league pain.

The anesthesiologist was there, and he decided to give Beck more morphine. The problem was, even a small dose on top of what he'd already been given, and Beck's unassisted breathing would be inadequate. So, while he was administering the morphine, I went to the head of the bed to work with what we call an ambu bag, a self-inflating rubber bag commonly used to mechanically assist patients' breathing by forcing air into their lungs. I think I kept at it for a half hour or so.

I awoke from this surgery with a serious case of the shakes. The pain was excruciating and it was everywhere. A simple touch felt as if I were being beaten with a two-by-four. It was like suffering some monstrous seizure, but I don't think it was a seizure in the sense that my brain was driving it. More likely, my muscles had just polarized and were firing out of control. Think of shivering, but with your muscles maxed out, not just a little tensed. Everything on full go, screaming.

Bub:

Besides my dad's physical appearance, he seemed to be doing all right after he got home from Everest. It didn't hit me how injured he was until after the surgery to remove his hand.

In the recovery room, I watched him lift his head, trying to see around him. He was shaking. His head was shaking from the effort, and all of a sudden his pain hit me.

The area on my left side where they'd taken the graft was covered with an occlusive dressing; that is, a kind of airtight film with an elastic rim. If you are lucky, the dressing stays in place, sealed and sterile, and everything is fine. But if it slips, as mine did, and air hits the skin, that is a serious ouch.

A vast area of me was exposed, and this acreage promptly was colonized by a drug-resistant staphylococcus. The infection was painful and messy. A goo started leaking out of me. My entire left side underneath the dressing turned yellow-green. Pus and bacteria. I smelled bad, too. Cleared the OR. Sent 'em out of the room gagging.

They put a drain in my side and left it there for six or eight weeks.

Meanwhile, the full body roar of rapidly misfiring muscle synapses finally quieted down until only my two amputations kept at it. When you cut through those huge nerves, every one of them starts screaming and won't stop. That lasted for a year. They just wouldn't give up. The sensation is like constantly being hit in the funny bone. It's disconcerting, an overwhelming jangle ripping right up both your arms.

When that finally subsided, a new sense took over—physical isolation. The hardest part of losing your hands is that you lose a huge amount of sensation. Forty percent of all your sensory input comes through your hands. These are serious input devices.

There are other obvious problems. You can't grasp and manipulate things. Remember my juggling kit? Very little of my gear survived Mount Everest, but when I finally got the stuff in Dallas, there was my juggling how-to booklet and the three little balls. I *had* to laugh at that.

Naturally, I thoroughly studied my new circumstance and learned there's a significant difference between surgical amputees, such as myself, and individuals who are born with no hands. They tend to adapt amazingly well. For instance, they can do astonishing things with their feet; there's not much they *can't* do.

However, they run into problems when they get to the age when arthritis sets in. They lose their limberness or develop back problems and can't put their feet where they need to put them.

For me, the sensory isolation of amputation is the worst part. I am acutely aware of it daily. I still have an intact palm on my left hand. One of my few sensory pleasures today is to feel the texture of Missy's fur as I pet her. It is both reassuring and kind of poignant. She is a constant in my life.

Still another surprise feature of my postdigital world has been my dreams. For whatever reason, they have become incredibly vivid since the surgeries. I'm aware of taste and smell now in my dreams. Everything is in full color, an incredible display. I have no explanation for this.

I'm also very much aware that I am dreaming. For example, I'll be riding a bicycle down a country road and I'll look down to see both my hands on the handlebars, working the gears and brakes. I don't step outside myself. I'm very much within my-self.

It's kinda fun. It means that for one third of the day, or what-ever time it is that I sleep and dream, I'm not diminished or handicapped in any sense. I run with the speed of a ten-year-old child, with no pain. I never tire. I'm a virtual Beck. Now, some-times, I don't have hands in my dreams. But when I do, I'm acutely aware. "Ha! I'm dreaming! See? I've got hands."

Greg Anigian performed two more procedures on my new mitt, to give it a little shape and integrity. First, he cut down a bit farther in the space between my thumb and the rest of the mitt, making it look more like a mitten. Of course, he needed a little extra skin, which he took from my crotch—without ask-ing.

I woke up after this surgery, looked down to see this incision across my groin, and cried out, "My God, is nothing sacred?"

The next and last procedure was to open a second incision, so that the mitt now would look like a primitively done fleur-de-lis. For this cut, they revisited my left side for skin.

I began about this time to inventory my body for areas as yet unoperated upon. There weren't many. In the end, only my right thigh would remain untouched. No one stuck a needle into it or anything. That had me concerned. I wondered what they were saving it for.

The last of the major medical projects was my nose.

It had been frozen pretty deep into my cartilage and bone. There wasn't much to save. But before the whole works was cut away, they took an impression of the original, using a piece of chewing-gum wrapper. When Greg Anigian went back to work, he'd use the wrapper to re-create my nose's contours.

In the interim, we had to improvise a way to keep my interior nasal passages moistened. The answer was a spray bottle. But since I now had no hands, guess who had to keep this little orchid's humidity at acceptable levels? Another chastening experience.

They grew me a new nose. First, a vaguely nosey-looking object was cut out of the skin in the center of my forehead. Then, using pieces of cartilage from my ears and skin from my neck, they shaped my new nares to give the whole thing some structure, and got it growing, upside down, on my forehead. I was careful not to allow the kids to take pictures of my upside-down nose, lest they sell them to *The National Enquirer.*

I also discovered that my unique deformity was a foolproof tool for sorting out my true friends. They all laughed their fannies off when they saw me. Everyone else was just polite.

The key was to wait until the new nose was fully vascularized. Greg scheduled me for one replant operation that he scrubbed when a look at the replacement part revealed it wasn't fully cooked.

Once he was comfortable with it, he cut the new nose loose,

swung it around on a pivot of skin, brought it down and sewed it into place. Then they stitched up my forehead.

At this juncture, I looked like some has-been pug, my nose a misshapen muffin below an odd little curlicue of skin. The final step was to take a piece of rib from my right side and attach it between my nose and palate to give the new feature some structural uplift.

I think they did a pretty fair facsimile of the real thing, and I was happy with my new nose, with a single reservation. Since the nerve supply remained intact when it was swung down, every time I'd take a shower and the water hit my forehead, my nose would itch.

Peach:

Beck and I were not communicating at all during this period, except on practical issues such as his health. There wasn't time. I was too tired and too stressed out and he was too sick. All I knew for a fact was that I did not plan to grab the kids and walk out, or send Beck to some convalescent center. At least not right away.

I did see evidence that he'd reformed himself, in part. There was that telephone call from Dr. Schlim's office, totally out of character. He was reaching for me, and I soon had a partial explanation why—the epiphany on the mountain. He also appeared genuinely contrite for all the pain he'd caused. What's more, Beck seemed to see the kids and me in a new light, maybe the light that awakened him on Everest. At this point he couldn't run away if he wanted to, but he didn't seem to want to.

I'd built up a lot of scar tissue over the previous eight or nine years, however. It was going to be very difficult, if not impossible, to trust him again. Even if Beck swore to me that he was a new man, it would be just words, not easy to believe. Although I didn't say it, or even think it at the time, he needed to prove himself. Action was necessary. If we were going to turn things around, it wouldn't be a big slow bend in the road. It would be a U-turn.

My brother Howie was the catalyst.

Howie was being his old reliable self: completely nonjudgmental, that incredible empathy. One time when we were all in Jamaica he befriended this scruffy character named Hedley, who became Howie's fast friend. Never mind that Hedley had a drug problem and that the security people wouldn't let him near the hotel, he and Howie were good buddies. Hedley doubtlessly was in it for a possible buck or two, at least at first, but Howie's goodness must have shone through. He even trusted Hedley with a credit card, and wasn't disappointed.

Howie flew to Dallas in his funeral suit the moment I called to tell him Beck was dead that Saturday morning, and arrived not long after we learned that Beck was alive. He took the children out for hamburgers, and kept an eye on things until he was sure my friends were providing us the support we needed. Then he said something funny about not liking crowds and flew home to his wife and daughter.

We continued to keep in close touch through Beck's constant medical crises into August of 1996, two months after the amputation, when Beck finally was well enough recovered for us to plan a brief family outing. Dr. Anigian delayed a scheduled procedure on Beck's left hand for three days, and we all flew off to

Fripp Island, a short distance up the South Carolina coast from Hilton Head, where Howie, Pat, and their daughter, Laura, joined us.

Within a day of our arrival Howie became seriously ill. I remember he walked up from the beach looking ghastly. "I really feel bad," he said. Howie's skin was white and he was sweating. He complained of chest pain.

There's a history of heart disease in my family. Howie was overweight and smoked most of his life. It seemed pretty likely to Beck and to me that he was having a heart attack.

Howard walked up to me ashen, with a sense of pending doom. He was sweating profusely. Even my old doctor books would describe that as looking an awful lot like a heart attack. I thought to myself, Howard, you simply cannot die on me here. If you do, I'm going to have to walk into the surf, and just keep going.

Peach:

We got him to a nearby hospital, where the doctors also believed a heart attack had occurred. But when they did a sonogram as part of their battery of diagnostic tests, they discovered a mass on Howie's liver. Next day, a CAT scan confirmed it: Howie had a primary cancer tumor on his liver, a hepatoma. It was big and the type of tumor that grows like a weed.

I reacted to this news much as I'd reacted to word that Beck was frozen dead to the side of Mount Everest. I went numb. I couldn't absorb it. My capacity for pain was momentarily over-whelmed.

I immediately knew Howard's likely outcome. I wanted to tell him that dying just isn't that hard. I'd done it once. I knew something about it. And I knew that for me, it would be much easier to face a second time. The fear is greater than the reality. If dying was really so difficult, there'd be some poor Bubba out in West Texas who couldn't quite get the hang of it and would be immortal as a result.

I never got around to telling Howard all this. Nevertheless, he managed his own death with a fair measure of grace.

Peach:

In Beck's case, we'd mobilized to rescue him, not realizing the impossibility of what we were trying to do. Now, I wanted a second miracle, a second rescue mobilization. Like an answered prayer, it materialized. This time, however, love and hope weren't enough to pull Howie through. Instead, it would be me and my family who were saved, in a wholly unforeseen way.

To my infinite amazement, Beck got involved.

Atonement definitely was on my agenda after Everest, but I didn't respond to Howie's needs as an act of expiation. First of all, I loved him. That was a big part of it. I'd been wrestling with the question Who do you love? and realized it was my family, the people who make up my existence. Now that I wasn't shielded by my goals, and had no other way to go hide myself, it was natural to respond as I did.

Also, I got involved with Howard because I was really trying to figure out how to actually *be* a different person. Peach and the kids always had been important to me, but I hadn't acted as if they were. In Howie's case, in the past I might have been sympathetic, but I would have left everything to Peach. Now I became viscerally engaged. I did not want to stand by and watch. I did not want to be immaterial in this.

Peach:

It began the moment Howie didn't feel well at the beach. Beck sat with him and talked to him. From then on he threw himself into it. Before, he might have said to me, "I can't possibly do this. I don't have the time." Now he was saying, in effect, "I'm on your team."

Howie was in a miserable state. He had this terrible tumor, and all kinds of trouble with his managed-care system, Kaiser Permanente. I did not hold out much hope for saving Howie, but I also knew that if we didn't move ahead in a hurry, nothing would happen. If there was anyone who should be able to help a person in his situation, it was a person in my situation. That's what I thought, at least. In truth, I was totally impotent. It was frustrating beyond all belief.

I couldn't get the system to give a shit if Howie was alive or dead. I called the head man at Kaiser Permanente *dozens* of times. I could never get past his secretary. He would not return my phone calls. When I did manage to get hold of a human there, he'd say, "I'm listening to ya. I'm hearing ya. I know where you're coming from. What can I do to help you?"

Of course he was going to do nothing. He was reading from a script. He didn't have the authority to do squat.

I'd ask, "Would you please have someone who can do something call me back?" And he'd just say again, "What can I do to help you?"

I called and called and called. I thought, These yahoos! I've never seen anything so insensitive, so *brutal*. Here's a man who's dying and they can't return my phone calls.

Peach:

Beck never would think of making a doctor's appointment for me or the kids. But with Howie he became quite aggressive. I remember he chewed someone out. Called him a miser and said he didn't care.

One of the first things Terry White and I discussed was a transplant. The Kaiser oncologist didn't even review Howie's films. Nothing. He walked into the room, looked at Howie's records, and said, "Oh, you have a hepatoma. It's bigger than five centimeters. We don't do transplants when tumors are greater than five centimeters." In effect he said, "You're gonna die. I could treat you, but it wouldn't make any difference, because you're still gonna die."

Kaiser diddled Howie around for a couple of months, and I believe that did affect the quality of care he received. I don't know, however, if it made a difference in his outcome.

Peach:

I took what Beck was doing as proof of his love for me and for my family . . .

I wanted to prove I could still make a positive impact on our lives.

Peach:

. . . but I still had to kick him in the butt a fair number of times. He and Terry would say, "There's nothing more to be done." I said, "Don't tell me there's nothing to be done. I live with a dead man, remember?"

I won't quarrel with that recollection. The fact is that Terry and I worked real hard trying to figure out some alternatives. Just because there was no happy outcome anticipated—remember, I also thought I was a dead man on Everest—the fact is that you ain't tryin' if you ain't tryin'.

Peach and I would have paid for the transplant; there just wasn't enough time to get one.

Our second idea was a major liver resection. We researched that one fully, too. It would have been a huge operation, and we finally saw that it just wasn't going to happen.

The third alternative, not a cure but a delaying action, was to embolize the tumor; that is, try to knock it down by cutting off its blood supply. Some success with this strategy had been noted in the literature. We tried it twice before turning to the last resort, chemotherapy.

Peach:

Howie lived four months after his diagnosis, from August of '96 to January of 1997. It was a very fast-growing tumor, but for the most part he suffered very little physical pain. He spent about half that time with us in Dallas, where Beck accompanied him on all his doctors' appointments. It felt like we had desperately sick people stacked up in every corner.

When Bub heard Uncle Howie was coming to stay with us, he voluntarily gave up his room and sort of camped around the house. Bub wouldn't give up his room for anybody. But he said, "If Howie needs to come here, then he should get my room. I'm moving out."

I also remember that autumn Meg had a special date. It was her freshman year, and she was wearing her first-ever short black dress. Howie wouldn't come down to meet the boy. He asked that Meg come up to Bub's room instead. When he saw her, he started bawling. He knew it would be the first and last time he'd ever see her that way, and he hadn't wanted to embarrass her in front of her date.

Howie faced his cancer with dignity. I can't remember the exact date of this, but I know we were all sitting in the den. Peach, myself, Howie in the rocking chair, Pat and their daughter, Laura. And it came to him right then that he was going to die. There'd been denial until that moment. Then all of us knew it, too, at that moment. We could fight a rear-guard action, but hope was gone.

It was an immensely sad moment. I could see Howie coming to grips with it. Then he rallied. He knew he had to be strong again for his wife and child. That was a hard moment.

Peach:

Howie's last hope was an experimental program Terry White found in Illinois. Only about half a dozen patients had been part of it. We knew it was a long shot.

When the call came that he had very little time left, Beck surprised me again. He easily could have said, "You go. I'll stay with the kids." But he didn't. He said, "I'll go with you."

I was at my microscope when Peach called the hospital to tell me that they didn't believe Howard could last the night. I said, "When do we leave?"

She said, "We need to be out of here in about an hour." I stood up from my desk, walked to the outer office and told my partners I was leaving, that I had to go to Chicago.

It was a silent flight. Chicago was bitterly cold. The wind blew a chill right through your body. The city was various tones of gray, with little if any color anywhere.

At the hospital, we passed through multiple security check-points on our way to Howard's room. We made it in time. Howard was lucid. He'd hung on, knowing his baby sister was coming to him for one last time. Pat and Laura were at his bedside. Each of us had the time to say good-bye to Howard, to tell him how much he meant to us, and I was able to thank him for all the times he stood in for me, had been the father figure I wanted to be but just wasn't any good at.

I told him I loved him. I embraced him and I kissed his forehead.

I've been told that people facing death can hold on by sheer dint of will, if there's something very important left for them to do. I believe this is true. Howard had held on, and now he was ready to let go. You could see him surrender to his exhaustion. He closed his eyes, slipped into unconsciousness. His breath became ever more labored and ragged. Then he was gone.

Peach and I left the hospital about four in the morning and went to our hotel. In all my time on mountains all over the world, I'd never felt so chilled.

Later that morning we flew back to Dallas. I had the window seat. Peach was beside me, her head on my shoulder, her hand on my arm. As the plane headed south in the light of the early morning sun, the rivers and lakes below us flashed up blindingly, brilliant gold turning to silver as the plane flew on.

The sparkle seemed to dance across the water, leaping to stay with us. I felt Peach's face against my cheek as we both stared out the window.

"You know what that is?" I asked.

"Yes, it's Howard," she answered.

That was exactly my thought. I could see Howard in that light, performing this last fatherly act, as he guided his baby sister safely home.

Back in Dallas, Peach asked me to deliver the eulogy at Howard's funeral, which would be held in Atlanta. Though I'm generally not at a loss for words, I did not want to do this thing. I loved Howard so much that I just didn't think I had the strength to deliver a eulogy without coming apart. But I also knew it was something I had to do.

Peach:

Most of the people who came to our house that May weekend in 1996 also sent flowers to Howie's funeral, eight months later. I don't know that I ever understood the purpose of flowers at such a time, other than a gesture of love and respect for the deceased.

But on this occasion, as we read their names on the cards and looked at all the lovely floral tributes, this same set of friends seemed to embrace us once again, their strength sustaining us yet again.

The pain I felt at Howie's funeral was all the sharper for the realization that my brother had been there for practically every important moment in my life. Then he had taken it upon himself to do the same for my children. Howie even came to my college graduation, which was no more personal (certainly not to me, anyway) than "Will the College of Arts and Sciences now rise?" At the time, Laura was a toddler, no more than two, yet

Howie and Pat drove a couple of hours with her so he could watch me graduate.

The occasions didn't need to be great or grand for Howie to take then seriously, either. For example, he once promised Bub he'd attend Bub's second-grade show-and-tell. The weather in Dallas started to go downhill in a hurry, and Howie needed to be in California the following day on business. He refused to leave, however, until he'd kept his word to Bub, and attended that show-and-tell.

Howie just understood better than most of us the importance of daily deeds, rituals and traditions, as opposed to grand entrances and exits; that it's the journey, not the destination, that matters in our lives. It does seem that we go to more funerals than weddings.

Peach also asked Meg to sing at Howard's funeral. Difficult as I felt the eulogy would be, I thought that paled in comparison to the prospect of Meg standing and singing in front of hundreds of people at her beloved uncle's funeral. Peach's friends suggested that this maybe wasn't a good idea. But Peach said, "No, Meg will do it, and she will do it for her Howie."

The funeral only served to remind each of us how central to our universe Howard had been. The easy part for me was to list the many academic honors and awards Howard had achieved throughout his life. The personal part was much tougher. I could see Howard reflected in the eyes of my family. They remembered Howard flying across the country to come see Meg in the lead in *Peter Pan*. They remembered Howard taking Bub under his wing, and giving my son a father's role model plainly superior to the one I offered.

Howard was a unique mix of intellect and intelligence with the outward look of the common man. He'd been a role model for my kids, and finally for me. I managed to get all the way through the eulogy with only the occasional pause to compose myself. During all this time, Meg sat silently in the front row, tears coursing down her cheeks. But as I finished, and it came her time to say good-bye, she stood up, dried her eyes and walked to the center of the altar, where, in a strong, clear, unwavering voice, she sang "Amazing Grace."

Each of us in that chapel was profoundly moved.

I once was lost, but now am found.

Peach wanted a second miracle, and it was granted. It just wasn't the one she expected. The year she'd given me to redeem myself had largely passed, and I was truly a different person. Howard in his final months had cast a lifeline to me, offering me the chance to save myself.

Thank you, Howard. You'll always be in our hearts. And in the end, that's the only thing that matters: those you hold in your heart, and those who hold you in theirs.

Epilogue

I'm pleased to report that I didn't kill as many brain cells on Everest as I feared. When I finally returned to my pathology practice, I made sure that everything I did was double-checked by one of my partners. It was sort of a long probation and apprenticeship to see if I still had it. Luckily, I did.

My key tools, my eyes and my brain, were working as well as ever. Foot pedals and voice controls partially compensate for my missing hands. The really detailed hand work, of which no machine is yet capable, is now done by my assistant, Kim Ledford.

The spiritual and emotional aftermath of Everest naturally is a far more complex question.

Many individuals have asked me how the Everest experience changed my perception of the spiritual, and did I pray on the mountain?

I was raised in a religious household, but as a young man I drifted away from spirituality, more out of apathy than any revolt or rejection of dogma. I felt that in old age I could return to these philosophical questions. Then I learned you can get pretty old, pretty fast.

I used to say that no, I didn't pray on the mountain. I was too busy trying to stay alive. Upon reflection, however, that answer was a shade literal. It conceived of prayer as a unity: a preamble, a stirring body of text and a close, preferably delivered from one's knees.

But if prayer isn't just words, but instead that thing you believe with all your heart at the core of your being, then I surely did pray. On Everest, more than any other time in my life, I had a sense of what was important to me, what I truly cherished.

I also was immensely comforted by all the people throughout the United States and the world who prayed for me and for my family. I learned again the power of prayer for those who offer it, and, certainly, those for whom it is offered.

I learned that miracles do occur. In fact, I think they occur pretty commonly.

I also now understand that humans are the toughest creatures on Earth. There's a reason we're at the top of the food chain, and it is not simply because we're a smarter cockroach. There's drive, determination and strength within each of us.

Most of us never have to tap into those resources. We live pretty easy lives, in contrast to the pioneers who settled the wilderness and explored far places. We may look back in awe at their strength and toughness, but they were no stronger or tougher than we. They simply had to live that life.

If you're going to come through an ordeal such as mine, you need an anchor. It may be your friends. It may be your colleagues. It may be your God. Or it may be, as it is for me, my family.

As spiritual matters go, I'm still very much a work in progress. Yet I have learned some things from this experience. It is impossible to go to Everest without being touched by the Buddhist Sherpas and their spirituality. Each morning you hear them offering their prayer chants for safety on the mountain. As you lie in the dark in your warm sleeping bag, the air is filled with the smell of burning juniper from their altar.

These are people who live their religion; it is part of their every motion. They don't just practice on Sunday morning and Wednesday night, but each hour of each day. If a religion is to have any meaning for me, it must not exclude such spirituality. It must encompass Hindus, Buddhists and Jews and Muslims and Christians and any other faith that shares my core values.

I think what truly matters in faith is not what you profess, but whether you live your faith's tenets. Ever the practical individual, if at the end of my days I discover there is no God, only the Void, I will feel I have lost nothing. Rather, by trying to be a better person—even if I commonly fail—I will have gained.

One source of strength in that daily battle is humor. Shortly after I was put back together, I was on a plane standing near a young woman struggling to place her baggage in the overhead. She glanced at me and asked if I'd be willing to lend her a hand.

Be still my heart! I was almost speechless with possible replies. Do I say, "I'm a little short at the moment?" Or "I gave at the office?" Or do you do as I did, say, "I don't really know how to respond. I'm simply stumped"?

As I began speaking before audiences about what occurred on the mountain, and how it has affected my life, I realized I get as much out of the experience as they do. You don't turn a fifty-something-year-old freight train around in a moment, even with an epiphany as profound as mine. Yet by telling the story, I remind myself of what is important to me. It gives me perspective that is so hard to achieve.

The other most common thing people ask me is whether I'd do it again. At first I'd think, What a stupid question! But as I considered at length, I realized that this is one of the deeper questions to be asked. The answer is: Even if I knew exactly everything that was going to happen to me on Mount Everest, I would do it again. That day on the mountain I traded my hands for my family and for my future. It is a bargain I readily accept.

For the first time in my life I have peace. I no longer seek to define myself externally, through goals and achievements and material posessions. For the first time in my life, I'm comfortable inside my own skin. I searched all over the world for that which would fulfill me, and all along it was in my own backyard.

All in all, I'm a blessed individual. Even better, I know it.

Peach:

Beck and I deal with each other on several different levels. The old Beck-and-Peach relationship is gone, but I don't yet know what will replace it. What do I believe? Do I open myself up to be hurt again?

While Beck was in the hospital a nurse approached him. She

said she was worried about her husband, who was climbing a peak in Colorado.

Beck said, "The view from the top is so good!"

I told him, "You don't say that in front of me. I'm done with mountains. I've donated. I gave at home."

In the summer of 1997, we got a letter about breast cancer survivors climbing in Antarctica, asking whether we'd like to contribute to their effort. One of my friends said, "You should write back and say I've already done my part—two hands and a part of a life."

Today, I do not consider my relationship with Beck to be fragile. Nor do I worry now that my anger might snowball or explode. I think my anger has turned to sadness for all that never was. Not for Beck and me so much as the fact that Beck missed watching his kids grow up. He lost his hands, but that's only the tip of the iceberg.

Meg:

I was annoyed that Dad was not around. I was upset. I guess lonely is a good word. But now that I'm older, I don't begrudge him the obsession. I understand what he did, and I forgive him. People get wrapped up in things like that and they don't realize what they are doing is wrong. Dad didn't until he got slapped in the face.

Bub:

I really admire my father's perseverance and determination, and his sense of humor. As I've gotten older, we also have had more and more common threads to share, like dirty jokes and R-rated movies.

Now he's become a man of the moment. He knows that when you love someone you should tell them because you don't know about the future. He's become a goofy Dad figure.

"You know what, son? I really love you!"

"Sure, Dad. I'll be home by midnight."

Pat White:

Beck's just a very fine person. He cares about people—however inadequately he expresses it. He's been wounded in his personal life, but he's still an acute observer. He translates that into humor.

Whatever the difficulties, there's great love there. They said Madan had a brave heart. Well, Beck has a great heart. And Peach is very brave in her way, too.

She didn't kill him.

Acknowledgments

When I first returned from Everest, there was a great deal of interest in having a book written from both Peach's and my points of view. In the early months following the tragedy on the mountain, such an undertaking clearly was premature. The emotional and physical pain needed to be confronted step by step, rather than in one cathartic leap. More than that, however, I had no idea how the story would end.

As the months passed, my interest in writing the story of the mountain actually diminished, as I felt the accounts by Jon Krakauer *(Into Thin Air)* and David Breashears *(High Exposure)* provided definitive documentation.

However, as I realized my life was coming back together, and my relationship with my wife was on the mend, my thoughts turned once again to the book project.

While the story of what occurred during those few days on Everest clearly is of interest, the story of what happened when I got back home and had to rebuild my life—redefine who I was—became *the* story for me.

There's no easy recipe for coming through hard times, but it is reassuring to know that even in the bleakest of moments, hope remains. Out of adversity, good things do happen.

It would be difficult to adequately thank the large number of individuals who have helped me struggle through, and hold on to body and soul. I wish to begin by thanking Peach, Beck II and Meg for loving me and staying with me and allowing me to change. And my parents, whose love has been constant. They raised their boys as best they knew how. Thanks to my brothers, Kit, and especially to Dan, who journeyed fast and far to be there when I needed him most.

To the many heroes of my story: David Breashears, Robert Schauer, Ed Viesturs, Pete Athans and Todd Burleson, who put their lives on the line for mine. And especially to Colonel Madan K.C., whose brave heart still astounds me.

To our guides on Everest: Rob Hall, Mike Groom and Andy Harris, who embodied the professionalism, character and sacrifice of mountain guides throughout the world.

To my team members: Doug Hansen, Yasuko Namba, Stuart Hutchison, Frank Fischbeck, Lou Kasischke, John Taske and Jon Krakauer—I treasure the friendships.

To the Sherpas who make all of this possible through their hard work and bravery: Ang Tshering Sherpa, Ang Dorje Sherpa, Lhakpa Chhiri Sherpa, Kami Sherpa, Tenzing Sherpa, Arita Sherpa, Ngawang Norbu Sherpa, Chuldum Sherpa, Chhongba Sherpa, Pemba Sherpa and Tendi Sherpa.

Also part of our team: Helen Wilton, who made us all wash our hands and kept us healthy, with the able assistance of Dr. Caroline Mackenzie, our Base Camp doctor.

To Senators Kay Bailey Hutchison and Tom Daschle, as well as Ambassador Sandra Vofelgesang, David Schensted and Inu K.C.

I would also thank the physicians, nurses and therapists who worked so long and hard to put me back together: Dr. Greg Anigian, Dr. Mike Doyle, Dr. Joe Sample, Dr. James Brodsky and Dr. Alan Farrow-Gillespie, as well as the physicians who assisted me on the mountain: Dr. Ken Kamler and Dr. Henrik Hansen.

I'm extremely grateful to my partners, Dr. John Esber, Dr. Charles Cramer and Dr. Wayne Taylor, for allowing me the privilege of returning to work with them, and supporting me and my family in the months before I was able to resume my duties.

Thank you, as well, to members of the Inner Circle, who were there through all the darkest days, and the Research Council: our friends Jim and Marianne Ketchersid, Terry and Pat White, and Jon and Sally Esber.

To Dan Lewis and his boys, as well as Deena Killingsworth and Jonnie Rohrer for their expert help with the press.

Thanks to Ken Zornes for coming by every Sunday morning with a box of doughnuts that helped me regain those thirty pounds of lost weight that Brent Blackmore helped me gain. And thanks to Cappy and Janie McGarr, my favorite Democrats.

And to the north Dallas power moms who fought like tigers to bring me home: Mary Ann Bristow, Cecilia Boone, Linda Gravelle, Victoria Bryhan, Maude Cejudo, Bobbie Long, Vickey Thumlert, Mary Ellen Malone, Ann Abernathy, Caroline Allen, Pat White, Yolanda Brooks, Liz Zornes, Jean Sudderth, Marcela

Gerber, Lisa Camp, Sue Washington, Sandra Barr, Barbara Lynn and Carolyn Kobey.

My appreciation to the many thousands of individuals who held us in their thoughts and prayers. This was a far greater comfort than you can ever know.

Finally, to Howard Olson, for all the love and inspiration he has given us, and for fostering that second, and perhaps greater miracle.

FREEFALL

Tom Read

Breakdown and beyond – The heroic story of one
man at the frontiers of human experience.

'This is *Bravo Two Zero* meets *One Flew Over the Cuckoo's Nest*. Tom
Read's story had me on the edge of my seat – and it also made me cry'
Andy McNab

On a flight from England to France in February 1994, Tom Read
looked across at his girlfriend and decided she would have to die.
He hadn't slept for eight days.

Harrowing and often hilarious, and grippingly unique, *Freefall* is the
electrifying true story of the former Red Devil's struggle to regain his
sanity and take control of his life, after his attempt to freefall into the
record books at the speed of sound found him tumbling into madness.
It is also a breathtaking journey through his past, from the freefall
displays for royalty, the attempt on Everest, the rigours of SAS
selection and covert operations in the Falklands and Northern
Ireland, to psychotic breakdown, terrifying flights of
paranoia and life in asylum at home and abroad.

'Extraordinary' *Mail on Sunday*

'A courageous book' *The Times*

'An incredible story: funny, sad and as breathtaking as a high altitude
skydive – *Freefall* takes you to the frontiers of human experience'
Cameron Spence, author of *Sabre Squadron*

Warner
0 7515 2659 2

SAVED

Tony Bullimore

'A cracking story' Libby Purves in *The Times*

The dramatic rescue of Tony Bullimore in January 1997 was the exhilarating climax to one of the greatest survival stories of modern times. When Bullimore's yacht *Exide Challenger* capsized amid the icy vastness of the Southern Ocean, he had been at sea for two months, competing in the Vendée Globe round-the-world race. Sheltering in a tiny air-pocket in the upturned hull, some 2,500 kilometres from the south-west coast of Australia, he now prepared for his loneliest challenge.

Saved takes us deep into the trauma of Tony Bullimore's ordeal, as he unfolds the events of his own past against the dramatic events that, hour by hour for nearly five days, were speeding him ever closer to his fate. Pulsating adventure story and poignant autobiography, *Saved* is the remarkable personal testimony of a true survivor.

'It is hard to think of a more terrifying thing than what happened to Tony Bullimore, or of a more inspiring story than the epic of his rescue' Geoffrey Moorehouse in the *Daily Telegraph*

'Bullimore not only relates his thoughts as each development unfolds, interspersed with flashbacks from his life, but he has also reconstructed the lives and conversations of his rescuers . . . He skilfully steers the chronology to an exciting climax' *Sunday Times*

Warner
0 7515 2334 8

NO ESCAPE ZONE

Nick Richardson

On 16 April 1994 Lieutenant Nick Richardson was shot down over the
besieged Bosnian Muslim town of Gorazde, his plane hit by a Bosnian
Serb surface-to-air missile. Lost behind enemy lines, his fate was
unknown to the outside world.

No Escape Zone is the story of Richardson's journey to the Bosnian
theatre of war and recounts in graphic detail the rigorous training, his
missions over Bosnia and the dramatic shootdown itself. But that was
merely the beginning. Picked up by Muslim forces, Richardson rapidly
learnt that nothing was what it seemed in the former Yugoslavia – war
had made it a place of medieval savagery, where allies became enemies
with frightening speed.

When the Serbs stormed Gorazde, Richardson and the crack SAS unit
with which he was now teamed found the Muslims turning against
them. A dangerous escape became their only option, because capture
meant almost certain death . . .

Warner
0 7515 3102 2

Time Warner Paperback titles available by post:

☐	Freefall	Tom Read	£6.99
☐	No Escape Zone	Nick Richardson	£6.99
☐	Saved	Tony Bullimore	£6.99

The prices shown above are correct at time of going to press. However, the publishers reserve the right to increase prices on covers from those previously advertised without prior notice.

_____ **timewarner** _____
paperbacks

TIME WARNER PAPERBACKS
P.O. Box 121, Kettering, Northants NN14 4ZQ
Tel: 01832 737525, Fax: 01832 733076
Email: aspenhouse@FSBDial.co.uk

POST AND PACKING:
Payments can be made as follows: cheque, postal order (payable to Time Warner Books) or by credit cards. Do not send cash or currency.

All U.K. Orders	**FREE OF CHARGE**
E.E.C. & Overseas	25% of order value

Name (Block Letters) _____

Address_____

_____

Post/zip code:_____

☐ Please keep me in touch with future Time Warner publications

☐ I enclose my remittance £_____

☐ I wish to pay by Visa/Access/Mastercard/Eurocard

Card Expiry Date

☐☐☐☐☐☐☐☐☐☐☐☐☐☐☐☐☐☐   _____